ABOUT THE AUTHOR

Tammy Cohen is an author and freelance journalist,
╷   ╷ London. She has written for numerous maga-
   ╷s a   national newspapers, specialising in human
ɪnterest stories as well as relationship, motivational
and celebrity features. Author of eight books, including the bestselling *The Day I Died*, *How I Made My First
Million* and *Deadly Divorces*, she currently writes for
Marie Claire, *The Daily Telegraph* and *Woman and Home*.

GANGSTERS' WIVES

Tammy Cohen

Quercus

For Otis, who can achieve anything

First published in 2010 by

Quercus
21 Bloomsbury Square
London
WC1A 2NS

A CIP catalogue record for this book is available
from the British Library

ISBN 978 1 84724 978 4

This book is a work of fiction. Names, characters,
businesses, organizations, places and events are
either the product of the author's imagination
or are used fictitiously. Any resemblance to
actual persons, living or dead, events or
locales is entirely coincidental.

10 9 8 7 6 5 4 3 2 1

Printed and bound in Great Britain by Clays Ltd, St Ives plc

INTRODUCTION

What is a gangster?

The blanket definition – a member of an organised gang of criminals – is as wide-reaching as it is meaningless. Robin Hood was a gangster. The fourteen-year-old from the inner city estate with a flick knife in his back pocket – he's a gangster too. Suicide bombers are gangsters, extended *Shameless*-style families who conspire to cheat the benefit system – all come under the 'gangster' umbrella.

Yet, ask the average person in the street to name a gangster and they'll say the Krays, or Al Capone. In the popular imagination, gangsters aren't scared teenagers under pressure to belong or politically motivated idealists, convinced that violence can be justified as long as it's for the greater good. The gangsters in our mind's eye are hardened criminals operating under a specially adapted moral code. They are both beyond the law and a law unto themselves. They are streetwise and ruthless and uniformly, unequivocally male.

Which leads us onto . . .

What is a gangster's wife?

She dresses in furs and carries a Prada handbag. She holidays in Mauritius and Marbella. She divides her mornings between the gym and the beauty salon and her lunchtimes between the Ivy and the Ritz. In the evenings, she chooses a designer dress from her walk-in wardrobe and goes clubbing in Essex, sipping champagne in the cordoned-off VIP section with her girlfriends and sisters. Her blonde hair is expensively streaked, her nails encrusted with tiny jewels. She is the underworld equivalent of a footballer's wife – a GAG to their WAG.

Or so we'd like to think.

In reality, of course, gangsters' wives are as diverse as the men they love.

Sure, some park their 4x4s in front of porticoed neo-Roman mansions on high-gated executive estates, but others wait out their days in squalid exile in poorly serviced tower blocks or live lives of blameless conventionality behind the windows of their suburban semis.

Just as there is no blueprint for a gangster, there is no such thing as a 'typical' gangster's wife.

The women featured in this book come from every walk of life, every age and social group. They are mothers and grandmothers, newly-weds and widows. They are housewives, lap dancers, students, writers, even kitchen tilers. They're shy, outspoken, resigned, aggrieved. In short, they are impossible to pigeonhole and as resistant to conformity as the men whose lives they've shared.

Some have been personally involved in their partner's 'activities' at one stage or another. Judy Marks went on the run with her drug smuggler husband Howard. She also couriered cash for him and travelled the world on a false ID. 'Carly' stayed up all night in her seven-bedroomed villa-turned-prison, counting hundreds of thousands of illegally gained euros for her drug baron boyfriend and acted as interpreter on drug deals worth millions. Jackie Robinson stole to keep her jailed married lover, Johnny Adair, in designer clothes. 'Donna' carried thousands of Ecstasy pills in her hand baggage just for the thrill of it.

Others operate a 'hear no evil, speak no evil' system, turning a blind eye to their partner's 'business affairs' in return for the lifestyle it affords, or just to keep the status quo. After all, what you don't know can't hurt you, right? And besides, it's a dog eat dog world out there, they say, and if it wasn't their men out there doing it, it would be someone else. Jennifer Courtney is phlegmatic about husband Dave's claim to have killed the man who'd just shot dead his companion. 'I'd rather someone else was dead than have to read Dave's obituary in the paper,' she reasons.

Then there are the nouveau wives, the ones who arrived on the scene after the event, piecing together their new love's wrongdoings from yellowing news-paper cuttings and faded court records. Anne Leach, who met husband Carlton when his friends paid her to lap dance for him, first confronted his violent past on the big screen at a Leicester Square premiere of the film of his early life. Lyn McKaig didn't believe her softly spoken new boyfriend Terry was once an inter-national cocaine baron – until he showed her his prison release papers.

So what's it like, living with a gangster?

Popular culture would have it that life as a gangster's moll is an endless whirl of lunches, holidays and char-ity functions. Try telling that to Becky Loy, forced to live in her car with her Romanian gangster husband, or Judy Marks who spent eighteen months in prison, separated from her kids, because husband Howard refused to believe they'd ever get caught.

Falling for a gangster means never knowing who's on the end of his phone, or when he's going to nip off unexpectedly, or if he's ever coming home. Prepare to do a lot of waiting around. Prepare to do a lot of prison visiting. Jenny Courtney professes to have worn out several vibrators waiting for her man to get out of jail. Former model and *Benny Hill* girl Maureen Flanagan clocked up thirty years visiting Reggie Kray and brother Ronnie in prison after making a deathbed promise to their mum.

Life with a gangster isn't about spending money just

as fast as he can extort it, it's about uncertainty, whispered conversations behind closed doors, long periods of separation without a definite end in sight.

Writing this book, I expected to meet doormats or prima donnas, women who'd traded their moral standards for a fridge full of champagne. I expected to find personalised number-plates and Rottweilers with diamond-studded collars, wall-to-wall jacuzzis and a big gaping void where a conscience usually goes.

Instead I found a group of women united only by their diversity and their links to men with a tenuous grip on right and wrong. In a vast but worn-out apartment in Mallorca, where the sun played on faded rugs and book-piled sofas, I met Judy Marks – who paid the highest of prices for loving her husband so unconditionally. In a tiny local authority flat in the East End, 68-year-old former Page Three girl Flanagan, still oozing glamour, held court about her years as confidante to the Krays, the photos on her walls a shrine to an era long passed. In a terraced house in Worthing, under the shadow of the gas works opposite, Lyn McKaig told how, after a Barnardo's childhood, she'd finally found, with boyfriend Terry, a place she could call 'home'. In a noisy bar in southern Spain, nervous, glossy-haired 'Carly' kept one eye on the door as she remembered the Faustian pact she'd entered into with her Irish gangster ex, who'd rented her a luxury villa that nobody could visit and splashed out hundreds of thousands on her clothes, but wouldn't allow her out to wear them. 'If you could have seen my soul, it probably had a designer label on it,' she told me wryly.

Researching the book, I stroked lapdogs, pored through photo albums and perched gingerly on a fur-covered swing in a garden-shed-come-sex-dungeon in the depths of South London.

I met women whose smiles warmed a room, and others who only realised they were crying when the tears splashed on the table in front of them. Some spoke with words spiked through with bitterness, others without a trace of regret.

Some had remarkable insights, others seemed, even years after the events, to be almost wilfully blinkered.

From Becky Loy who was facing homelessness for a second time when I met her in a dusty Fuengirola café, where plastic tables lined the traffic-fume-filled main road, to Anna Connelly, now a busy working grandmother, but still fiercely protective of the memory of her fiancé Viv Graham, gunned down in a Newcastle street on the very last day of 1993, the women in this book gave generously both of their time and themselves.

Shameless self-promotion? A chance to set the record straight? A means for revenge? Absolution? Apology? The savouring of old memories? Whatever the motivation, the stories were told with honesty and without conditions.

INTRODUCTION

Behind every good man is a good woman and behind every gangster is a woman with a good story to tell. And here are some of them . . .

JENNY COURTNEY

Dave Courtney holds the dubious title of Britain's number one celebrity gangster. According to his own website, his pedigree is impeccable: 'In his time, Dave has been shot, stabbed, had his nose bitten off (they sewed it back on) and has had to kill to stay alive himself. Dave Courtney has been involved in debt collecting, minding clubs, assault, contraband and murder, to name but a few things.' Dave has also been referred to as the 'Yellow Pages of the Underworld' due to his criminal connections. He's been up in court on numerous occasions – sometimes appearing in front of the judge clad in a court jester's outfit – yet only been found guilty once, after attacking five Chinese waiters with their own meat cleaver. On trial in 2001 alongside corrupt policeman Austin Warnes, accused of plotting to frame a London woman by planting drugs in her car – a charge he flatly denied – Courtney was so incensed by suggestions that he was a police informant that he attacked Warnes in the courthouse. He knew that being labelled a 'grass' put his and his family's lives in danger. Dave's flamboyant public life is matched by his private life. He and his wife Jenny have talked openly about swinging, and once had a break-up so nasty that she accused him in court of wife beating.

The first time I came across Dave and Jenny was at a wedding in the early 1990s. Jenny, an eye-catching black woman, sported a leather corset, shaven head and studded dog collar. Dave was the best man and presented the happy couple with a gold-plated knuckleduster. A week later, Dave turned up at our front door with a big unsmiling friend in tow. He hadn't come to compare wedding photos either. Someone at our address had been writing dodgy cheques and, completely coincidentally, he'd come to collect. Well, thankfully it turned out that someone at a very similar address *had been writing dodgy cheques*, but it was a close call.

Fast forward nearly two decades and I am walking uncertainly down a nondescript road in Plumstead, South London, convinced I've got the wrong address. Surely Dave and Jenny can't live in a place like this? You'd expect such unconventional characters to be living it up in a penthouse pad in Soho. And yet here in Plumstead the houses appear to be bog-standard terraces, running on, one after the other, in an unbroken line . . . until I round a bend, and suddenly there standing in front of me is undoubtedly, unmistakeably Camelot Castle, home of Mr and Mrs Courtney. Twin majestic gateposts flank the entrance from which fly two flags of St George. The top of the house is fringed with battlements, *between which life-size models of American civil war soldiers peer bravely out, muskets at the ready. The side of the house is covered entirely by a mural of Dave as King Arthur, surrounded by his trusted knights of the Round Table. Dave comes to the door wearing just a shirt and explaining that he's only just got in from a party the night before. I follow him to the kitchen, where Jenny is making tea for the builders who are fixing the conservatory where the ceiling seems to have fallen in. Where Dave is larger than life, in every sense of the word, Jenny looks tiny and slightly on edge. Dressed in androgynous black T-shirt and jeans, she doesn't look any different from when I first saw her at the wedding seventeen years before, except that instead of having a completely shaved head, she's now sporting a tuft of hair on the top. She looks tired, but still nowhere near her thirty-nine years. With her slight frame, it's hard to believe she's a mother, let alone a grandmother. Leading the way into the living room, which is painted black and dominated by a giant portrait of Dave, complete with angel wings and gold-leafed knuckleduster, Jenny is polite, but weary, as if there are plenty of other things she ought to be getting on with – like tiling a kitchen or two (she has just qualified as a kitchen tiler). As she starts talking, however, her reservations seem to melt away. She's unguarded, funny and disarmingly frank. She takes me on a tour of the house, finishing up at the end of the garden where, guarded by a life-size model of a guardsman in a sentry box, the Courtneys have built their very own sex dungeon. Inside there's a red velvet throne, a pole-dancing pole, a fur-covered swing and a variety of objects with ropes and buckles attached that I decide not to ask too closely about.*

Sometimes people get lost in the Dave myth. They see him on the telly and they think he's this or that, or completely unapproachable. That's so far from the truth.

Dave is who he is – he's never anything else. He never tries to be. Some people are one way in public and another way behind closed doors. Dave is just the same wherever he is. There's no show with him. And he's the funniest guy I know. Everyone wants to be with Dave because wherever he is, that's where the fun is. The police raided the house a while ago and divided us all up into different areas of the house. A few of us were inside, and we were all clamouring to go outside with him because we knew that was where the fun was. He's like a breath of fresh air.

In the face of adversity, Dave laughs his bollocks off.

Growing up, I'd never met anyone remotely like Dave. It just wasn't in my radar. I grew up in south-east London, Woolwich – Greenwich. I'm a twin and one of fourteen kids. Growing up with so many brothers and sisters, there's always sibling rivalry. We had some amazing fights, but I wouldn't be without them now.

My parents were very strict. My dad is a mechanic, my mum is a housewife and a devout Christian. My mum used to have to take us to church – we hated that, sitting in the van with our hats on, having to make a dash from our front door to the van. She still won't step into a pub, or smoke or tell a lie.

I used to think my dad was moody, but now I look back on it, by the time he was thirty-nine years old he had fourteen children. There's not enough hours in the day, not enough days in the week, not enough money coming in. He just had a lot going on. He was doing the best he could.

When there are that many kids, there's no house big enough. We always had a five-bedroom house, but I never had a bed to myself. Not ever. Not even when I moved out.

I left school at fifteen without passing any exams. It was a bit scary really – me and my twin sister Julia didn't have a clue what we wanted to do. We ended up going to college to study community care – elderly, children, mental health, care in the community. We were really into rap music and we also started MC-ing in local clubs.

I got together with a guy and had two children – Genson and Drew – when I was still in my teens. I didn't know at the time but the kids' dad had mental health issues. It was only after I'd got with him and had Genson that I discovered he was a paranoid schizophrenic. He'd had a tough life. Once, when he was younger, he apparently walked into his flat, walked straight through and jumped off the balcony.

We were always breaking up and then getting back together. He was quite violent and I'd break up with him, but he'd still hang around until finally I relented and took him back.

When Genson was about seventeen months old and Drew was four months old, Julia and I were asked to MC a club called the Fitness Centre in Southwark Bridge. It was 1989 and we were booked through a promoter we knew. I didn't know it at the time but Dave was the owner of the club. I'd never even heard of him.

When we arrived at the club, I went to put my jacket away in the cloakroom. All of a sudden, I felt a tap on my shoulder. When I turned round, there was this guy standing there wearing a Stetson, a waistcoat and cowboy boots with spurs. He had the bluest eyes I'd ever seen.

The minute I saw him, I fell for him. He looked so lovely. I was completely smitten, hook, line and sinker.

'Hello, mate,' he said, smiling.

I could hardly speak. I mumbled 'hello' and walked away with my heart pounding.

A short while later, he came over to me and offered me a fag. I thanked him, and as I turned to move off he stopped me and said: 'I don't know if you're married or if you've got a boyfriend or what but I'm going to have you.'

I was really embarrassed. I didn't know what to say and made some silly joke and he said: 'I don't just mean as a shag, I mean I'm going to marry you and have children with you.'

All the time, his bright blue eyes were just boring into me. I just squeaked: 'All right then.' And that was that.

At that time Dave was married, with three kids. And even though I wasn't really with my kids' dad, he was still hanging around. A few weeks after we met, Dave asked me, 'Do you want me to make him go away?'

By that stage, I knew enough about Dave to know he was serious. I said, 'I'd love him to go away, but I wouldn't want you to hurt him.' He said, 'Leave it to me.'

I don't know what happened after that, but that man never bothered me again. I don't know what Dave did to make him 'go away', but I saw him around a couple of times and he wasn't dead and he wasn't limping, so that's good enough for me.

Dave's marriage was another story. He says himself that his ex didn't do anything wrong, and she's a really nice lady, but she was a casualty of his lifestyle. I was the tail end of a long line of women so I could imagine what she'd had to put up with. It was hard though. I have a lot of time for Tracey.

I'd already fallen in love with Dave by the time I started to find out about what he did for a living, and by then it was too late. I just didn't care. At that time he was a big shot – debt collecting, running the doors – he had 500 blokes working for him. There were phone calls day and night, he was a really busy guy.

I'd only known him a little while when I saw a programme on the telly about him. It was called *Bermondsey Boy*, and followed him as he prepared to go to court for ABH and tampering with witnesses, and then as he was acquitted. I was watching it and I thought: I'm sure that's that geezer from the other night. He looked a bit different, but I was sure that was the bloke I'd met. He was wearing the same ring.

It probably sounds mad but the programme didn't put me off, even though it showed him turning up on doorsteps with a baseball bat in his pocket. As far as I was concerned, I thought I'd already seen everything of him I needed to see. I was so smitten.

The effect he had over me was so powerful, I can't even explain it. For example, I used to suffer from really bad toothache. I'd be immobilised with it, lying in agony at my sister's house, which was like a meeting place for everybody. Then Dave would come round and immediately the toothache would be gone. Just like that. My sister would be looking at me saying 'Hang on, we've been running around for you all morning because your tooth was so painful'. Then the minute Dave left again, the toothache would be back.

We moved in together about four or five months after

we met. I was living in a flat with absolutely nothing. When Dave made my kids' dad 'go away', he took everything with him – the kids' beds, everything. I just thought, I don't care. I'd rather be left alone and have nothing.

As far as my kids are concerned, Dave is the only dad they've ever known. He brought them up. He was the one who took them to the doctor when they were ill, picked them up from school. Dave and I have got a daughter together, Courtney de Courtney, who's now eleven, but he always treated my oldest two as if they were his own.

Dave was the kind of dad who made everything fun. If he was giving them a bath, the whole flat would be flooded, but they'd be having the greatest time. He'd cook, but use loads of food colouring so there'd be blue mashed potatoes and purple beans. There was always loads of mess and mayhem with Dave's parenting, but always maximum fun too.

The thing that would probably surprise most people is that Dave isn't just a comedy dad, he's really considerate too. Really thoughtful. My daughter Drew was an early developer, and was a bit embarrassed about it and one day, without even mentioning it to me, Dave took her out shopping and had her fitted for her first bra. I wouldn't have known what to do, but he whisked her off to M&S and came back with hundreds of pounds' worth of underwear. She was delighted. I'm not quite sure what the woman in the shop thought – Dave's white and my oldest kids are both black. But that didn't bother him. He just wanted Drew to feel comfortable. That's the kind of man he is. He's a care-bear.

Dave is so soft-hearted. One time we were coming out of the Ministry of Sound nightclub and got chatting to this old bloke whose son worked on the door and who used to make a little bit of money finding legitimate cabs for punters in return for a couple of quid here and there.

Anyway, this old guy was really worried one night about a poll tax bill he'd received but he couldn't pay. He was terrified he'd get a debt collector at the door. He said, 'Dave, could you have a word so that they don't come round?' Dave took the bill off the geezer and said he'd see what he could do. Then, later on, he asked me to go into the post office and just pay it for him.

A couple of weeks later, the old guy comes running up to Dave outside the club, all smiles, and said: 'Dave, I don't know who you know, but I got a letter saying I've paid that bill, and I know I haven't paid it. You must know some powerful people.' Dave never let on he paid it, because he knew that would just embarrass the guy. Instead he just said, 'Whatever you do, don't tell your mates.'

That's the side of Dave I fell in love with. Of course he has two sides to him, and there's the side I don't see when he's at work. But it's like he says, a bricklayer isn't a bricklayer when he comes home. Dave puts on that 'pay the money back' head when he needs to but when he comes back home, he's the most relaxed, lovely, funniest person. Right from the start I knew what he did for money, but he could always justify it.

One time, this geezer had robbed his partner who'd put £50,000 into this business and the geezer had put it into liquidation and opened up again across the road, almost exactly the same thing. Dave didn't like that. He said to the guy who'd been swindled, 'He's legally robbed you. That's not right. I'll get it back for you, but I want half of it.' Well, half of £50,000 is better than a whole of nothing, isn't it?

Minimal violence is what Dave's about. You look at Dave's face, he's got that kind of a look that says you don't want to mess with him, so that way he doesn't have to get nasty. Dave went into that bloke's house in the middle of the night. He walked past the kids' bedrooms, walked into the master bedroom, leaned over the wife and tapped the geezer on the shoulder, woke him up and said: 'You know you owe the rest of the money, don't you? Pay up because next time I won't do you the courtesy of waking you like this.' Then he went away. No violence, nothing.

He says that if he does it that way, the wife does the rest of the work for him. She says, 'Pay the guy the money, for God's sake – that man just walked into our house, past our children. Pay him.' Course it's not always that cut and dried. He's kicked the wrong door in before – he just says 'Sorry, here's the money for the door.'

I know what Dave's capable of, and it doesn't scare me. The fact that he's killed someone in self-defence doesn't scare me. I'd rather he'd have done that than he's the one lying dead. It was in Amsterdam, Holland and he was being paid to look after someone – he was the muscle, the deterrent. Before he left on that job one of our mates had given him a gun with six bullets in. Dave asked if he had any more and he said, 'Listen, mate, you've got six there. You miss, you're in the wrong fucking job, mate.'

The bloke he was supposed to be looking after was shot right in front of him. Dave told me afterwards: 'I've seen dead people before, but I've never had someone I've been talking to seconds before, lying on the floor in front of me. I knew the next thing would have been me. I've got the thing in my pocket that'll make sure I get home to my missus. I'm sorry but I'm using it.' And I'm glad he did. I'd rather someone else was lying dead than have to read Dave's obituary in the paper.

The police never really forgave Dave for being so cocky when he got off on that *Bermondsey Boy* programme. When the court case was over he was asked, 'Did you do it?' and he said, 'No comment – of course I did.' They'll never leave him alone.

He's been up in court so many times. The worst was 1996. It was Friday 7 June – I remember because it was my birthday the following Monday.

Dave was at home. His friend came by the house with another boy called Mark, and said he was going to pick up his mate from the airport. It was a nice warm day. Dave said, 'I'm not doing anything, I'll come with you.' He only went along for the ride.

He was wearing tartan shorts, a T-shirt, shoes with no socks and carrying a mobile phone. It wasn't like he was dressed to go anywhere or do anything. He was in the wrong place at the wrong time. The bloke that they were going to pick up had imported cocaine.

Dave didn't know that. All Dave had done was unknowingly introduce the two people who'd come up with the plan in the first place. Then he'd gone along to the airport just to keep his mate company. It was nothing to do with him.

But they were all nicked. Apart from the boy Mark, who'd gone to the airport with them. He'd nipped off to get a coffee or whatever, and come back to find them all getting nicked, so he ran off.

First I knew of it was Mark standing on the doorstep saying, 'They've all been nicked.' I just thought: Oh no no no. Straight away I knew that out of all of them that had been nicked, Dave would look like the one in control, the Mr Big, even though he really wasn't.

I had to wait until the Monday to visit Dave, which was my birthday. I thought he was being held at Wormwood Scrubs. I picked up the wives and girlfriends of the others who'd been nicked with him and we drove up there. But unbeknownst to me, when Dave had come out on the wing at Wormwood Scrubs earlier that day, all the bad boys had been shouting out and cheering him, which hadn't gone down well with the authorities. So he'd been put into solitary, then whisked down to Belmarsh. I only found that out once I got there. All the other wives went in but I had to go and sit round the back on the grass.

I was so down in the dumps, so depressed. I hated every one of the wives because they'd seen their blokes and I hadn't, even though I knew it wasn't their fault at all. I felt gutted that I'd missed Dave and the next visiting wouldn't be for a few days.

I couldn't wait to drop the others off and go home to be miserable by myself, but as I turned the corner and drove by our local pub, the Albion, I noticed something from the corner of my eye. It was like a sea of red just visible through the windows and door. As I got closer, I realised the entire pub was filled with red roses. From where he was in prison, Dave had still managed to send all these roses for my birthday – the pub was overflowing with roses, they were coming out of the door there was so many. That melted me. That's the kind of man he is.

We soon discovered that Dave was looking at seventeen years if found guilty. I couldn't let myself think about it. I wouldn't have been able to carry on if I had and I knew I had to remain focused – for Dave, and for the kids.

He served a year on remand before the trial. He was in Belmarsh which was a Category A. I visited him three times a week. The other co-defendants were at Wormwood Scrubs. I'd go pick the wives up and take them to visit.

During that year he was inside, I was his arms and legs. I wanted to do my bit to help Dave with his case. It was lonely though. I've never wanked so much in my whole life. I got to know me intimately if you know what I mean. I got to know the workings of a vibrator. I learned to take it apart and put it back together again. I can make it work without batteries!

When the court case came up, I was a witness so I couldn't go into the court until it was my turn to be called. I asked a friend who could do shorthand to go to court for me and take notes so that I could stay on top of things.

In court, they showed footage of them all at the airport. Dave looked at it too and said, 'Listen, I treat you as professionals, so now you treat me as a professional. I'm in security. Do you think if I thought there was over a million pounds of cocaine in that suitcase I'd be standing way over there? Are you nuts? I'd be *in* the fucking suitcase. I promise you, that is not how I'd look after a suitcase like that.'

The prosecutor tried to say that Dave was responsible because he introduced the two people who came up with the plan. Dave went: 'Oh really? If I introduced that lady customs officer to that man over there, and later on they meet up and have a shag and she gives him Aids, am I guilty of murder? I introduced them, he put his cock in her, does that mean I'm guilty of that?' As soon as he said it, everything went quiet and I was thinking: Oh no, no, no, babe, you've blown it. Then the judge said to the lawyer: 'Well, answer Mr Courtney.' I was so relieved. I thought: Thank god.

When he was acquitted, it was the most amazing feeling, just indescribable. He had everything stacked against him. Each of the jury members had an armed guard going home with them. There were armed guards on the public gallery, helicopters, the works. If you were a member of a jury, you'd think if a man needs that level of protection, he's got to be guilty. They're not going to pay all that money for someone who might be innocent. But they acquitted him.

Out of the five who were in court, only Dave was acquitted. We went to a hotel and decided to try for a baby then and there. We'd talked about it while he was in prison, but I'd said, 'I want to have a baby with you, but not if you're in here.' I remember having a shag and doing a handstand.

Our daughter Courtney de Courtney was born nine months later. She's white, I mean really white. When she says, 'Mum' you can hear the wind of people's heads turning. Trust me, she's white.

We got married 17 March 2001. We'd gone out to Joey Pyle's wedding in Las Vegas and Dave proposed to me there. It was romantic. It was wicked. You know how weddings make you go a bit emotional? Well, just before Joey walked his wife out of the chapel, Dave turned to me and asked me to marry him. I said, 'Yeah!' He said, 'We can do it tomorrow.' I said, '*Really*?' I had no doubts whatsoever.

We got married the very next day. It was wicked. I took my vows holding his bollocks in my hand the whole time. No kidding, I was holding his penis – because if there's anything sacred enough for me to take a vow on, it's that.

It's hard for the kids sometimes because Dave is who he is. You can understand parents being dubious sometimes about letting kids come round to our house because of what they read about Dave in the papers.

I've tried talking a bit to Courtney about it, explaining it's every parent's right to protect their children. I've said, 'You're a lovely girl, but you might be friends with someone whose parents' perception of your dad isn't good. If they don't invite you round it's because of what they've read about your dad.'

The worst time was when Dave was up in court over the bent copper case and people thought he was a grass. That was awful for Courtney because suddenly there were no parties, no nothing.

You'd invite kids round and they wouldn't be allowed. I can understand – the chances were someone was going to shoot him so why would you want your child round my little girl's house?

That was a truly awful time. The copper at the centre of it was called Austin Warnes.

He was asked by a private detective he knew to plant cocaine in his client's wife's car so that the client would win custody of his kid, as they were divorcing. We didn't know any of this. One day we went to meet Austin. We met him on the common and he said: 'I need your help, mate.' He told us he'd been seen talking to Dave and he needed to come up with a reason. He told Dave that if his boss called him in and asked what he'd been doing, he should just say he was giving Austin information about a load of drugs being sold by two women. He said he'd made up some names so the stories matched – and one of them was this woman, the mother of the child. Only we thought they were just made-up names.

The boss did pull Dave and ask him and Dave told

him what he'd been asked to. Because of that it looked later on like Dave set this woman up.

When the police found drugs in the woman's car and she was pulled in, she said, 'Hang on, I think my husband is involved here.' When the police were asked why they searched her car they said they were acting on the information of an informant. They were asked to name the informant. Of course they said Dave.

The police had the detective bugged so they heard when he and Austin hatched the plan and they were watching them from the off. Austin was saying 'can you say this', 'can you say that', so when the police pulled us in, they *knew* we didn't know anything.

When they arrested Dave, we were on our way back from Manchester. They plotted to arrest everyone involved at the same time – six a.m. They didn't bank on the fact that Dave was going to be picked up at six o'clock in the morning by a driver to go to Manchester to do 'An Audience With . . .' We went, did the gig, went to the Cavern, all that, and we were on our way home, having a shag in the back of the car. I thought: something's weird. Then I saw the lights and thought: not again. They just came and nicked him. Didn't say who they were, just came and nicked him.

When I came home, I tried to locate him, but none of the police stations would admit they had him. In the end after I threatened to report him as a missing person, they told me 'he's incommunicado'. I didn't know what they were nicking him for or where they'd taken him.

About three hours after I'd got home, they raided the house. I had a photo I'd taken of Dave and Austin sitting on a bench. They were watching us at the time – they had surveillance up trees and lip-reading experts on hand – so they knew that I'd taken a picture of that meeting. But what they didn't know was that Dave was actually recording that meeting as well. He said: 'Right, why am I doing this?' and Austin said: 'To help me out of a spot of bother, Dave.' It was all on tape.

I think that's what the police were looking for – the photo and tape of that meeting which were evidence that Dave didn't know what was going on. So when the policewoman started questioning me about the common, I said, 'I know what you're looking for and it's not here. Dave's not an idiot.' I went up to my room where I knew the picture was. I said I needed to get a new nappy for Courtney, and I slipped the picture down the inside of my jeans, right under where I had Courtney on my hip, and I kept her there the whole time. They didn't find it.

The tape wasn't in the house. The tape was elsewhere. When I went to see Dave I asked him what I should do about the tape and he told me to give it to police, but to make sure I made copies first. So that's what I did.

The price for being a grass in this life is you get shot.

Dave could have got shot because of what Austin and the others tried to say about him. It's a good thing people know Dave and they trust him, or that would have earned him a belly button in the forehead. It's nasty.

For a couple of days while Dave was in the nick, a friend of ours got his minders to stay with me. These men were all round the house. But when Dave came home he said, 'Nah. Fuck that. I've done nothing wrong. No one is going to come and shoot me. If I've informed on someone, there'd be someone in prison saying "Dave grassed me up for this".' If anyone ever said to Dave, 'I heard you're a grass', he'd say, 'I've heard I'm a grass as well, but who did I grass up then?' And nobody ever had a name. They'd say, 'I just heard.'

I know Dave wasn't a grass. When the geezers were out there, minding us, I didn't feel like we were in danger. My mind was on Dave. But when Dave came home and sent them away I felt even better. I felt safe because I knew he hadn't done anything wrong.

When the case came to court, Dave warned the authorities not to put him in the dock next to Austin. He said, 'If you put me in the dock with that guy, I'll knock him out. Don't do it.' The first day of the trial, Dave came in dressed as the court jester and that Austin was standing in the court waiting room. Dave just went right up to him and knocked him out. I was shouting at Austin: 'You're a liar. You've been around my kids in my home and you've still done this to us. Why?'

All that stuff made me feel so bad for Dave, even though he was found not guilty. He should have been patted on the back, not made out to be the bad guy. But you know I'm glad I know things like that go on in this world. I'm glad I'm well informed. I feel enlightened by that knowledge, not threatened.

There's always something going on with Dave. Sometimes I listen to my mates stressing about what to wear and I think: 'Oh, if only that was my only concern. The luck of only being worried about that . . . I know I'd get bored in the end, but it'd be so nice not to worry about him.

He's been hurt a lot. One time he got shot in the ankle when he was working on the door. It was a drive-by. Dave was in the hospital. He had his boys positioned at the end of his bed, and two boys outside the ward. The police came and offered him an armed guard. Dave said, 'What can your people do that mine can't do?' They said, 'But we've got armed guards.' Dave said, 'The only thing that your boys have got that my boys haven't got is a bit of paper saying they're allowed to use their guns.'

But the doctors have a duty to their patients. They're not going to put their patients at risk by having a few of Dave's burly mates guarding him. They patched Dave up and sent him away. It never healed properly.

But that's nothing compared with his accident at the end of 2001. Well, I say accident, but I think the police tried to run him off the road. He was in a coma for a month. I believe their sole intention was to stop Dave going to court and opening up a can of worms.

They pit-manoeuvred him, clipping the car so that he lost control on the motorway. They're trained to do that. That's the only time in history that they haven't been able to retrieve any video footage off that motorway. Never before has it been known but the cameras weren't working on that side of the road that night. Really? What a surprise.

First I knew of the accident was a notice stuck on my door telling me to contact the police. They didn't put it through the door, they stuck it to the outside of the door so I didn't see it until I left the house later that day. And even then I just thought: Oh no, he's been nicked again. I rang the solicitor and said, 'Dave's been nicked again.' The solicitor told me to ring the police, so eventually I did and was told he'd been involved in an accident. I said, 'Sorry?' I just couldn't get my head round it. It just didn't seem real.

They said he was down at Darent Hospital in Dartford. When I got there he was in the resuscitation room. I knew it was serious then. I thought: Oh God, what's happened to him?

The doctor came out of the room and said to me: 'The police keep coming in trying to do blood tests and what have you. I'm trying to keep your husband alive. That's my job. I appreciate they have to do their job, but they have to let me get on with mine.'

The minute he said that, my head started whirring and I was thinking about what really had happened.

When the doctor took me in, I was really shocked. In Resuscitation, there are beds in the middle of the room and you can walk all the way round. I was standing right at the head of the bed, looking down at Dave's face, so he could see me upside down. He'd had a tracheotomy but was still conscious at this stage. I leaned down and he whispered: 'I've really hurt myself.' It was awful.

Then he went unconscious. Though we didn't know it then, he would be in a coma for a whole month.

I was still in shock and started looking at his notes. They'd resuscitated him by the side of the road for half an hour, got him into an ambulance, raced him to hospital, and taken him straight to Resuscitation because they lost him again. It was horrible. He was so badly injured. He had a fractured skull, broken ribs, punctured lungs and his pelvis was completely shattered.

Dave had said to me a long time before that if he was ever on a life-support machine, he'd want me to turn it off. He'd watched friends of his get ill with things like MS and he'd said to me, 'Babe, I don't care if you fall out with my mum and she never speaks to you again but do not have me resuscitated to be like that. If I'm like that, turn me off. Do not leave me like that.'

While he was in the coma, he was read his last rites. Later Dave told me he could hear what was going on. He kept coming in and out of consciousness, but he could tell what was happening. He could feel my tears on his arm and hear his mum crying and hear this man saying 'last rites' and he said it was almost like he was inside his own body trying to run to his arm to make it move. He said he was remembering how he'd said to me, 'Don't let them do that to me. Turn me off.' And he was thinking: Don't do it, babe.

To be honest, I didn't get that far. I didn't think about him not making it, or about switching him off. I didn't think any of that. I just knew he was going to come round. Don't ask me how. I just knew it.

Courtney and I stayed in the hospital the whole time he was in the coma. Courtney slept under his bed every night. So I was there when he came round. It was amazing, like watching someone being born again. Dave has these gorgeous blue eyes – he'd woo your mum with those eyes, believe me – and he opened them. He had these red bloodshot whites and those same bright blue eyes. He kept opening them and shutting them.

I was so excited I can't even describe it. But I think I'd seen one too many Hollywood movies. I said, 'Babe, you need to communicate, I'm going to write out the alphabet.' I got a piece of paper and wrote it out in big red letters. Then I said: 'As I point to the letters just blink at me when to stop.' But when I'd got an 'M' followed by a 'Z' I thought: Hmm . . . there's something wrong here.

After he regained consciousness, he was on morphine because of the pain and it made him hallucinate. He thought the hospital was prison. One day he rang me up at home saying: 'Get me my trainers.' Then one of the men who was visiting him also rang saying, 'Dave wants his trainers.' I said, 'What does he want his trainers for? He can't walk. He's got no pelvis, it's completely shattered. He's like Bambi. He's not going anywhere.' But it was the morphine. The nurse said, 'Bring the trainers. It'll shut him up.'

It traumatised me. He was hallucinating and I didn't know what was real and what wasn't real. Morphine does that, it's a mind bender. But no one ever explained that at the beginning.

There was a boy in the hospital, a paraplegic. He'd had a crash in his car and he'd gone through the windscreen and his whole body had twisted. He was in a wheelchair. His dad saw me struggling with what was happening to Dave and said, 'Listen. It's the morphine. Me and my wife had to go through this. Our son saw us bursting into flames. We thought he'd been mentally scarred, we thought he had mental problems but it was the morphine.' That really helped me.

Later that same night, a nurse had moved me away

from the bed so she could do something, and I'd fallen asleep. Then I was woken up with a big crash. That was Dave making his great escape from prison. He'd got up, all Bambi-like and crashed to the ground. He had blood all over his face.

I was so happy when Dave came out of the hospital, but it wasn't plain sailing after that. Far from it.

In 2003, me and Dave had a breakup which lasted more than four years. We had a fight and he fell on me and I got broken. I went to the hospital. Despite all the stuff that was said and written, I was never a battered wife. Never. I'm the first girl out of all those fourteen kids. There were a load of boys before me, so I grew up knowing how to fight. I can stand up for myself.

He didn't beat me up. We were having a fight and he fell on me and as he's bigger than me, he hurt me. It's as simple as that. But to my family it was something else.

I went to the hospital. When I came out of the X-ray room, my mum and dad and my brothers and sisters that could get off work were all there. My dad started crying. My mum said, 'How do you think I feel, seeing you here?'

Now as far as relationships go, I never run to my family complaining about what someone has done. The way I see it, you spend most of your relationship trying to get your family to love your bloke in the first place. And my family did love Dave, but seeing me in the hospital shook them up.

When I came out and saw their faces, I took the chip out of my phone and threw it away so Dave couldn't contact me. And that was my mistake really. Having no contact meant his imagination ran wild and I'm still trying to mend things from that.

I went to stay in this caravan for a few days with my sisters and my mum right after the fight and it was all negative, negative, negative. I know they were worried about me, but it was doing my head in. I thought: It's still Courtney's dad you're talking about and I still love him. I know I can't wipe my bum, I know I'm a bit busted up, but I still love the geezer.

I knew if I went back to London it would be more of the same – all negative, and I couldn't face it so I rang my mate up in Ashford and he arranged for me and Courtney to go and live up there for a while. But he's a working man, his wife was working. I come from London and I was dying up there. Courtney would be at school and I'd be stuck there on my own. Fridays I'd go to get her early. The minute she'd get out of school I'd go down to London.

When I'd been in Ashford about four months, I was told Dave was making plans to go to live in America and take Courtney with him. With hindsight, I shouldn't have believed it unless I heard Dave say that with my own ears. But I did. I was advised that the only way to stop him was for me to formally accuse him of beating me up and I'm sorry to say that's what I did. I made that accusation of domestic violence because I was afraid of him taking Courtney away. And that's the only reason. If I could take it back, I would.

As a result, he was nicked. To get off the domestic violence charge, he got loads of people to come in and say this, that and the other in court. It was hurtful stuff and it wasn't true, but he got off with it.

It put a big wedge between us. Dave knows why I did it now, but at the time it was awful. I went out on a few dates in the time we were apart, but men would always think I wanted to hear how hard they are, and how fantastic. They felt they had to live up to Dave. And I'd think: I don't want to hear that. You're not him, so don't try to be. It was horrible. It was really horrible.

We didn't see each other at all in that time. He didn't see Courtney either because he didn't want to risk her becoming a pawn between the two of us. That was a big thing. I didn't offer for him to see her, and he didn't ask.

It changed once we moved back to London. Courtney started doing this drama class with another kid from school, and me and the other mum used to take it in turns to take them. One day the other mum rang me and said, 'I'm not sure, Jen, but I think Courtney's dad is two cars behind us. What should I do?'

I didn't have time to think. I said, 'She needs her dad to come and put his arms around her and tell her he loves her', and before I'd even got off the phone I could hear Courtney shouting 'My dad, my dad', and going nuts. When the other mum rang back, she said, 'They're both sitting there sobbing.'

We've been back together eighteen months and I'm so happy. But that doesn't mean everything has settled down now. The police will never stop trying to pin something on Dave. I think it's got a lot to do with that bit at the end of *Bermondsey Boy* where he was asked: 'Did you do it?' and he smiled at the camera and said: 'No comment.' It's stuck in so many people's minds.

If anyone comes near us, the Old Bill are on them. My daughter came to visit us the other day and her car got stopped and searched. She's never been stopped and searched in her life.

The police have the keys to our house in Plumstead now. Dave gave them a set so they wouldn't have to keep kicking the door down. They haven't used them. They keep sending letters saying, 'Can you come and collect your property?' We've also had Dave's eyes painted onto the roof of the house so that the police can see them from their helicopters and know he's watching them.

The constant police attention means Dave couldn't do anything naughty now, even if he wanted to. He's too well known. But I'm not naive enough to promise he'd never do anything again ever. There's people out there who have got scars on their bodies through being with Dave and protecting him. If they came knocking on the door and said, 'Dave, I need help', I don't expect Dave to say no. No way I don't. I'd expect him to go and do what you do as a mate. Because that's what mates do. What am I going to say – that he shouldn't have any mates?

People have this misconception that we're rolling in money. Not a chance. The money is a myth. Sure, Dave has had money in the past, but he isn't money-driven and it's all gone. He walks around like royalty with nothing in his pocket. We get occasional big bits of money from Dave's books or whatever, but because we spend so much time without any, it just goes right away. The trouble is you can't borrow a fiver when everyone thinks you're a fucking multimillionaire.

I'm a qualified tiler, and I have a props hire business, although it only just breaks even. When Dave made the film *Hell to Pay* we had to hire guns from an armoury. Because there were loads of extras needed, we got our mates to bring their mates so there'd be loads of people milling around that we didn't know and after each shoot, there'd be a gun missing. To be honest, it was only to be expected, boys will be boys and criminals will be criminals. But it was embarrassing having to tell the armoury – and expensive having to pay for new ones. So I set up a props company myself – Prop-a-Job. We know lots of people who make films where they need a sword or a gun, or Dave uses them on photoshoots. Problem is that because the directors are usually our friends, and the films are low budget, the business has never exactly been profitable. Contrary to what people believe, we're not rolling in it. We get some money from my tiling work, or Dave does the odd 'Audience With'. But that's it.

But the police even try to stop that. I know what they think, that it's glamorising crime, but I'm sorry, people want to know about that stuff. Dave will be booked to do 'An Audience With . . ., in a club or a pub and the pub owners will get a call saying 'cancel that show or you won't even get a TV licence, much less a drinks licence'. And then Dave gets a call from the pub to say the Old Bill have said they can't put on the show.

So we stay home – Camelot Castle in Plumstead. It's a great house. The sex dungeon in the garden was built before the kitchen – get the priorities right. The dungeon is part of our lives. We use it regularly. When Dave turned fifty In 2009, we had an all-night party in there with us and four other people. It was wicked.

The swinging is just fun. I used to think it would improve trust between us, but now I don't think that any more. Now it's just something we do for a laugh, I don't think about it any deeper than that. We don't have an open relationship though. We swing together.

The house is very tongue in cheek. The living room is decorated with guns and weapons, but it's not supposed to be serious. Above the fireplace in the living room there's a painting of Dave with angel wings and a knuckleduster. The painting has got Dave's DNA in. The bloke cut Dave and mixed the blood with the pigment for the paint so that the painting can never be copied. It's got real gold on it and diamonds, flawed diamonds.

Everything about Dave is over the top. Everything is larger than life. I'm the one who has to be boring and sensible sometimes and take things seriously, but I don't mind that. I can deal with it. I just get on with it quietly and leave him to his thing.

He wears the trousers in our house, but I tell him which ones to wear.

Update: Since our interview, Dave has yet again been back in prison, this time facing a charge relating to possession of firearms.

JUDY MARKS

Judy Marks spent nearly three decades in the shadow of her charismatic husband, Oxford-educated international drug smuggler Howard Marks. At one point Marks was so successful he was estimated to be trafficking a tenth of all the marijuana smoked in the world. He and Judy travelled the world in style on false passports, living under different aliases and sometimes on the run, until the birth of the first of their three children led her to seek out a more settled existence. While Judy tried to keep the family on the straight and narrow, Howard carried on his smuggling activities, despite being warned that he was under constant surveillance. The result was that, in 1988, he and his wife were arrested at their Mallorcan home. Howard spent seven years in prison in Spain and the States, Judy eighteen months, separated from her children, who suffered terribly.

Two decades on, and now divorced from Howard, all traces of the jet-set life Judy once lived as the wife of Mr Nice (Howard's favourite alias) have vanished. The car she picks me up in on a Palma street corner has seen better days. Inside, its ashtray overflows with cigarette butts. The views from her top-floor apartment are staggering, but the furnishings are more about shabby chic than interior design, more about comfort rather than fashion.

Judy herself is hospitable and sharply funny, but visibly nervous, and constantly questions whether what she has said makes her sound too embittered, too angry. With Howard now a fixture on the UK celebrity-speaker circuit, and a film about to come out about their lives together, it's clear Judy feels that she was in a sense sacrificed for Howard's new-found fame; yet, fiercely protective of her children, she worries about maligning the father they still adore. It's a delicate balancing act.

Sometimes nowadays I find myself thinking: I wish I'd never met Howard Marks. That shocks me, because I never used to think like that. But these days I find myself thinking it more and more. Because even though we were together for the best part of three decades and I loved Howard unconditionally, there are some incidents you just can't forgive. And more that you can't forget.

If you'd have told me I'd ever feel this way when we first got together in the early 1970s, or even when he returned home from jail in 1995, I'd have thought you were mad. I was so besotted by him.

And inevitably the thought then strikes me that I wouldn't have my beautiful, wonderful children if I hadn't met him. And we did have an amazing connection, which many people spend a lifetime seeking. We were soulmates.

I'd first met him at a dinner party in Brighton in 1970 when I was just sixteen and he was ten years older. I was terribly attracted to him but he was with Rosie, his girlfriend at the time, so I didn't think anything could happen, particularly after I'd got stoned and passed out. Seriously uncool. Strangely, Rosie told him after this dinner party that he would end up with me. He thought she was completely crazy.

At first I didn't know what he did for a living but afterwards I heard through the grapevine that he was a drug dealer. It didn't bother me though. I wasn't particularly shocked by what he did. I'd been dabbling in the drugs scene since I was thirteen or fourteen so it all seemed fairly normal.

I came from a big family – three boys and three girls. We were considered quite well-to-do and lived in a big house in Stafford where my father was the managing director of an electronics company. But I think all us children were quite rebellious, which is where the drugs thing came from. We smoked dope and hung out with people who dealt it, so there was always criminality around, although we didn't perceive it as such.

We were an unconventional lot and out of all of us

children, only my younger sister has stayed out of jail. But the rest of us? I guess we weren't the most law-abiding of children.

When we moved from Stafford to Brighton the rebelliousness became more exaggerated – a bigger scale of what we were doing in a small town in Stafford. But to us it was normal life. No one was shocked by it. It was the seventies and the era of nonconformist, boundary-pushing youth.

My older brother Patrick became involved in Howard's 'activities' which is how I then went on to meet Howard and Rosie at that dinner party.

Howard was incredibly charming – still is. He was also very good-looking and everyone adored him. When he walked into a room, everyone would stare. He just had bucket-loads of charisma, which he has never really lost, although now that I'm older and wiser I can see through it and see how he uses it to manipulate people.

After that dinner party it was as though everyone was talking about Howard, although it was probably because I was listening out for his name. Then he got busted and everyone was talking about that too. But, as I say, to me what he did wasn't unusual. I guess the fact that Patrick knew him normalised it slightly.

By the time I got together properly with Howard a couple of years later – the night before my history A level, in fact – I knew all about what he did and I found it interesting. If Howard had been a different kind of criminal, it would have shocked me, but then he wouldn't have been him.

The whole thing about dope dealing at that time was that everyone involved was just normal. It was just a bunch of overgrown students, really. They were all university graduates, all nice people, who just happened to make their money from dealing dope. They all drove BMWs, the same model, but different colours. Even today I can't look at a BMW without thinking about a dope dealer. Dope dealing then was very different from how it is now – without all the professional criminal elements.

Years later, when Howard came out of Brixton prison and started hanging around with Dave Courtney types, I hated it. I wouldn't have them in the house or anything because to me they were a different type of person to the people Howard had 'worked' with in the early days. These were people who do nasty things. Howard and his friends weren't like that at all.

Even though I was a rebel and took drugs, I'd never really done anything 'bad'. I never even nicked sweets from Woolies which is probably quite unusual. I didn't even know that's what people did. To me there was a big distinction between what Howard and the rest of us were doing and 'bad' things other people did. I certainly didn't think we were criminals.

We had great fun in the early days, even though Howard was on the run when we got together. He had been due to face charges, alongside four others, of conspiring to export hashish into the US and had mysteriously 'disappeared' before the trial began. When we got together he was living under a false ID. We were broke a lot of the time during those years. We lived in a tent, for God's sake. It wasn't as if he was rolling in money, whatever people might have thought. He was spotted by the *Daily Mirror* in April 1975, and found his photo on the front page under the headline 'The Face of a Fugitive' so we had to leave London. We borrowed £500, bought a tent and lived in it for months. Luckily it was a beautiful hot summer that year.

I knew our life wasn't 'normal' but I thought it was fun, and who wanted to be 'normal' anyway? I'd always been a bit of a rebel, rejecting the idea of a nine to five existence, and at that age you don't really think ahead. Or I didn't think. I didn't consider the consequences. It just felt like being a little bit naughty, nothing more. All our friends were very respectable and they all thought we were a little bit naughty and found it exciting that they had 'naughty' friends. It was just that, nothing more, certainly not organised crime.

I became aware Howard had started getting bigger when the Colombian Operation was proposed at the end of the 1970s. Some Colombians wanted Howard to smuggle fifty tons of Colombian weed into the UK. I thought that was just mad. At that time, fifty tons was a huge amount in England. In the end they brought fifteen tons in through Scotland – still an enormous quantity. I was involved in the conversations in that I was there and I knew what was going on and thought it was crazy, even though it was my own sister who introduced Howard to one of the key players involved, an American who owned a yacht-chartering business based on a small island off the coast of Scotland.

But still I didn't really worry because they were all such nice people. Everyone we hung out with were nice and respectable. And none of them were going 'tut tut', so I reasoned it must all be all right. If I bothered to reason at all.

Howard wouldn't have anything to do with the hard drugs in those days, nothing to do with cocaine. It wouldn't have been in Howard's character as he was at the time. And that just reinforced my view that what we were doing was just a little bit 'naughty', not really criminal. Just smuggling a harmless, beneficial substance.

My feelings started to change when I had children. Before then I was just as naughty and unconventional and up for doing anything as Howard was. Then, in 1977, I got pregnant with Amber and thought: hang on. I was living on a false passport then and, even though we were travelling all over the world, flying first class and staying in fantastic hotels, I wanted to go home. I wanted to go back to England, reclaim my real identity and basically not put myself in the firing line any more.

From that point I did try to live a much more low-profile life – well, as much as it's possible to do while living with the biggest drug dealer in the world, as they called him at the time.

Once I had the kids, what Howard was doing and how he was making a living started to become a worry. I had my second daughter Golly (real name Francesca) while he was in Brixton prison awaiting trial after the law had finally caught up with him, and he promised he wouldn't do it any more. I wanted so much to believe him and we actually got married on 22 July 1980, while he was in prison. I felt optimistic that things were going to be different, but in the event it didn't take him long to go back on his word.

After he'd gone on trial and been acquitted – which I felt was so lucky – I was very, very disappointed that Howard then went back to crime. I was really, really upset. I thought it was crazy, given all the publicity his case had generated. We argued a lot about it. It would always be 'oh, this is the last one', or 'don't worry, I'm just the middle man'. There would always be an excuse: 'It's all right because . . .'

I wanted to believe him. I remember very, very well, being in our old house and looking at him and saying, 'You're never going to fucking stop, are you?' He said, 'I will . . .' but he never did. Until it was too late.

Howard never came right out and told me he'd started up again after his acquittal, but I'm not stupid. I knew enough about the business by that stage. You hear something on the phone and think: I know what you're talking about.

And I hated it. The reason I objected to it was I didn't want Howard to be arrested. It was about what it could do to our family. It wasn't a moral judgement. I didn't think there was anything wrong with hash smoking or smuggling. I didn't think he was hurting society in any way.

When he came out of Brixton, Howard set up various legitimate companies. The travel business actually did quite well. Now, of course, I can't believe he'd ever have made a success of anything because he's been so useless at seeing things through, but back then I still had my rose-tinted specs on and believed what he was telling me. When the money started coming in, he'd explain it by saying: 'Oh, we made X in the travel agency business.' How was I supposed to know if that's where the money really came from? His parents and sister fell for it. Probably because we all wanted to believe it.

When I finally realised beyond doubt he was back at it, and I couldn't stop him, I said to him, 'I don't want to know the details.' That was very hard because half the time the other people involved would come up and start talking to me about it. I'd just say, 'I don't want to know, I don't want to know.' I said, 'I don't want to be put in a position where I have to choose between my children and grassing anyone up. Please don't tell me anything.'

It probably sounds silly, but I don't think I ever gave him a final ultimatum, despite everything. I'd say 'please stop it or you're going to get caught', but I never said 'stop it or I'll leave you'. I loved him too much. Plus I wanted to provide a stable family unit for the girls, who absolutely adored their father.

It really worried me though how much the whole dope dealing scene had changed. When Howard went to Brixton prison for those two years and met all these bank robbers, he thought he was doing them and society a favour by telling them they should become dope dealers and then they wouldn't have to go round doing armed robberies. He retrained these guys. The next time Howard and I went to Thailand it seemed that half of Brixton prison had joined him there. In a way, one could say that Howard began the trend of having 'bad guys' join the dope business in the UK.

In the mid-eighties we moved to a house in Mallorca where we had a very normal lifestyle. In fact the teachers and other parents were really shocked when we were eventually arrested. They really thought Howard just ran a travel business. We weren't ostentatious, we didn't drive flashy cars, or drip with gold. We had a big house but it was in a little Spanish village.

Yes, we used to travel a lot. We used to eat out in nice restaurants. We always used to fly first class and we stayed in the best hotels – but then he was in the travel business, so it wasn't exactly surprising. And in Mallorca our life was very ordinary. The children never missed school, they were always on time, and I always attended the school parent evenings and meetings.

Howard was away for ten days every couple of months. The rest of the time we were just an ordinary family. All the kids knew was that he had a travel business which is why we travelled so much. By that stage I had three children – Amber, Golly and a new baby, Patrick.

It became increasingly obvious that Howard was going to get caught because we were told by a friend of ours, an American called Tom, that he was being investigated by the US law-enforcement agencies. We still don't know exactly who Tom was working for. He claimed he was with the CIA and with the DEA [Drug Enforcement Administration] and he showed us documents showing they were following Howard. They were going to make him out to be the biggest dope dealer in the world and then bust him and bust me too, Tom told us.

He told Howard: 'You're at the centre of this investigation. This is what they're doing.' Then he said: 'They're going to arrest Judy as well.' But Howard just wouldn't believe it. He said, 'They can't do that. She hasn't done anything.'

He kept this denial up in the face of all the mounting evidence. He just couldn't admit any chance of being caught. I was with him when Tom came and knocked on our door with all this paperwork and showed it to us both. It completely freaked me. They were very official papers and the amount of information and details they contained was phenomenal. But I still couldn't get Howard to stop what he was doing. What could I do? Walking out wouldn't have saved me. The American authorities didn't have any evidence against me, but they were determined to get me on any pretext. The first piece of paper I saw accused me of racketeering dope since 1970 or something – when I was fifteen!

The truth is that the things I did do, like couriering hundreds of thousands of pounds of cash around for Howard – all happened before the children were born. There were two different stages in our life together: me actively being naughty and me wanting to be straight because of the kids.

In the new film they've made about us, they have me travelling on a false passport with Myfanwy (Howard's daughter from his relationship with Rosie) who, in the film, they've made into my daughter. I said, 'I really object to this because I never travelled on a false passport with the children.' They said, 'Well, we'll cut Myfanwy out altogether then.' I said, 'You can't do that.' So they left that bit in, but it's completely inaccurate. Once the kids were born, I kept my head down and toed the line completely, which was why it seemed ludicrous that the Americans might be out to get me.

Tom showed us the documents about Howard and me being investigated about two years before we were actually arrested. After that, whenever we heard from him, my name never came up. It was just Howard who was mentioned. Howard kept thinking that by paying Tom more and more money he could keep them away. I didn't trust Tom and thought he was just taking the money off Howard. Howard wouldn't have it. Tom wouldn't do that to him.

The problem is, Howard is completely narcissistic (although at the time I failed to recognise it). He thought no one would ever grass him up and no one would ever catch him out. He really believed he would never be caught, so even knowing that he was being watched, he still carried on making deals.

He had made friends with the infamous Lord Moynihan in the Philippines. Even though he was told that Moynihan was secretly working for the DEA, Howard carried on dealing with him. How crazy is that? That's what I mean about him being an egotist. He simply couldn't believe he was being set up. Howard even sent Moynihan over to see my brother Patrick in Miami to talk about money laundering. Patrick hadn't been involved in anything dodgy for years but that's what led to his arrest and to all of us being arrested because, before that, Craig Lovato – the DEA agent who had made it a personal crusade to hunt Howard down –

couldn't get any state to bring the charges against us. They had to find a crime in a particular state. By Moynihan being introduced to Patrick, it gave them the evidence they needed to bring charges in a Florida courtroom. I have never been able to understand why Howard put Moynihan in touch with Patrick and never said 'Oh, by the way he's working for the DEA'.

The arrest, when it eventually came on the 25th July 1988, was horrific and unexpected. In the period leading up to it, everything seemed to have quietened down. There weren't too many phone calls from Tom. Howard had actually said 'That's it, I'm not doing any more'. I thought finally his smuggling days were over. But suddenly the police were swarming over my Mallorcan house and the children were caught up in a horrific nightmare.

'Mummy, this is the worst day of my life,' Golly told me. She was only seven and didn't understand what was happening.

I believed I would be released later that day. I thought it was a mistake and I'd be out. I was stunned when I arrived at the police station in Palma and was told that though I had committed no crime in Spain, I was to be held awaiting extradition to the US. I was being accused of involvement in a series of cannabis importations totalling 700 tons and dating back to 1970, when I was just fifteen. I was flabbergasted.

I didn't think they could possibly convince a Spanish

court to extradite me. I kept thinking they'd let me out. The lawyer was also convinced they'd release me. When I found out I was going to be moved from the prison in Palma where I was being held to Madrid, leaving my children behind in Mallorca in the care of my younger sister Masha and her boyfriend, I just couldn't believe it.

It was awful. You can't describe it. You feel so helpless. You're the mother, you're meant to be there looking after your kids and you're not.

My lawyer in Mallorca had gathered witness statements to prove what kind of mother I was and why the children would suffer if I was separated from them for an extended time. I still have the handwritten letter from the headteacher at the children's school which avows: 'My judgement of Mrs Marks is very clear: she is a most caring parent who has devoted her personal attentions and very considerable skills and intellect to the upbringing of her children, intellectually, morally and socially.'

And yet none of that seemed to carry any weight. There's an expression 'pain in my heart'. I never knew what it meant until I was arrested and sent to prison. Then I had it all the time – twenty-four hours a day, seven days a week.

I was taken to the notorious Yeserias prison in Madrid. Howard was in Madrid also, at the top security jail, Alcala-Meco. Apart from seeing each other at court hearings, we were allowed a three-minute phone call every Saturday.

Sometimes I'd lie on my bed in prison and feel really angry with Howard. I'd rant and rage at him in my head and think about the mess he'd got us into, and about what he'd done to my family. Not just me and the kids, but my brother Patrick and my other brother George, who was also wanted by the law because of his connection with Howard. But then I'd see Howard, or talk to him on the phone and I'd just feel terribly sorry for him. That's a joke isn't it? I'm lying in jail, my children are parentless and I'm feeling sorry for him.

The prison in Madrid was a shock. Before I got there I had heard stories of the violence and dreadful conditions. But nothing had prepared me for the reality. Yeserias was originally a plaster factory. During the Spanish civil war it became a military hospital. There were still shell holes in the walls.

It was then Madrid's only women's prison with an official capacity of 369. When I was there it held over 640 plus fifty children under the age of six. All but four of the three hundred foreigners in the prison were there for smuggling drugs. And drugs were rife in the prison. They were run and controlled by five or six Nigerian inmates. The Spanish were their customers. The Spanish junkies were like packs of wild dogs. Waiting to pounce, to get what they could to feed their heroin habits.

I slept on a thin mattress in a dormitory crawling with cockroaches. Life in there used to make me think of the Jewish ghettos I had seen in old war movies. It was nothing like any kind of prison I had ever seen.

The only thing that kept me going was the hope of getting bail and being allowed to go back to my children. But each time I allowed my lawyer to convince me it was going to happen, I was disappointed. At first I thought I'd be home for Amber's eleventh birthday in October 1988. When that application was denied, I was sure I'd definitely be out by Christmas. After each refusal, I'd imagine the disappointment on their faces and feel as if I was drowning in blackness.

Seeing the kids in prison was both terrific and awful. I would look forward so much to seeing them, to holding them, smelling them and hearing their voices – yet I was always aware that in too short a time they would be torn from me again. Because of a shortage of money, they were only able to travel up to Madrid every three months. So those visits were extremely precious.

Patrick, as he was under six, was actually allowed into the prison to spend the whole day with me. I was greatly distressed by his behaviour. He'd thump my face, scratch my eyes, pull my hair and bite me. I was riddled with guilt. My sister Masha, who was looking after them back in Mallorca, looked tired and complained of a burst eardrum. I can't remember what reason she gave for how it happened.

Maybe I should have seen the warning signs, but I was completely blindsided when I received a telegram at the prison in February 1989. It was from our family doctor back in London. Golly had been taken to see him when she fell ill while visiting friends over half term.

Judy, sorry about the circumstances. You must remove the children from your sister's and her 'amour's' care immediately or I will have no choice but to have them put in care.

Getting that telegram was horrendous. It came as such a shock. And I was helpless to do anything. Masha's boyfriend had become a junkie and had been beating her up the whole time, although she wouldn't admit it. The kids had witnessed everything and had also suffered terrible neglect.

My sister hadn't wanted to get Patrick out of his cot while the boyfriend was still around so the poor little thing had just stayed there for hours on end in a darkened room screaming. His sisters weren't allowed to go to him.

And yet no one had told us. I still don't understand why no one did anything. Why hadn't the school said anything?

I soon realised that people had noticed but weren't quite sure what to do. My younger brother Marcus, who'd moved to Madrid to help me with my case, hadn't wanted to say anything because he didn't want to worry me. Apparently the family doctor in Mallorca had also been to the house and found the boyfriend unconscious, kicked him and said, 'Shit, he's still alive.' So it wasn't as if people didn't know what was happening, but no one had wanted to tell me.

It was only the family doctor in London who'd seen Francesca and after an hour's conversation with her, sent me that telegram.

Can you imagine how that makes you feel as a mother? I was full of anger and loathing against myself for not being there to protect my children.

Immediately, I got in touch with my older sister Natasha, who flew over from the States with her two little boys to take over the care of my children.

After that, I was even more angry with Howard. I can remember lying in my bed wishing I could hit him. But still whenever I saw him, I'd forget those feelings and feel sorry for him.

Getting the telegram in prison was one of my lowest points. The other was when another co-defendant's lawyer came to see me and told me I was facing fifteen years mandatory. That was pretty awful. I felt as if my head was about to shatter into fragments. I thought: I'm not going to get back to my kids until they're grown up.

After a year in prison in Spain I volunteered to be extradited to the States because it seemed the quickest way to get out. The translator at the Spanish court told me 90 per cent of the judges in the high court in Madrid didn't think I was guilty and didn't think I should be extradited. It was pure pressure from the Americans that kept me in prison. I volunteered to be extradited because otherwise the fight would have dragged on and on.

Also, I'd found out that my brother Patrick had received a three-year sentence, much lower than we'd feared. I thought: Well, if they've only given Patrick three years, I'll only get three seconds, maximum.

I'd thought of going over before his case came to court but Patrick asked me not to because if they had me there, they could have put pressure on me to grass him up. I think the judge at Patrick's trial realised Patrick hadn't really been involved to the extent of Howard and Ernie Coombs (the main man in the US). Patrick had been out of that whole thing for years and it was only when Howard sent Moynihan over that he got involved again.

But even though I'd been told I had a good chance of being released, actually arriving in the US was very scary. My moods went up and down as I projected ahead, thinking of the best outcome – that I'd be let off – and then the worst – a long prison sentence in a US jail.

Howard followed me out to America, having lost his extradition fight, and worries about his fate also weighed heavily.

I had moments when I thought: I'm not getting out

of here. At first I wanted to plead not guilty to the ludicrous charges that had been made against me but the prosecutor threatened that if I didn't plead guilty, the charges would be filed under new laws. This meant that if I was found guilty of conspiracy, I'd face a mandatory sentence of fifteen years with no chance of parole.

Realising they had the power to do that, I pleaded guilty of importing hashish into the US. Finally, in December 1989, after I'd been in the States six months, I was sentenced to time served. In other words, I could leave prison. But even then it wasn't as simple as it seemed. I was released and then immediately re-arrested for being an illegal immigrant and sent to this really awful jail in downtown Miami where I stayed another week or two. I ought to have been ecstatic at the prospect of my imminent release, but my relief was tempered by my horrible surroundings, and by the fact that I'd had to say goodbye to Howard just before leaving the federal prison, not knowing when I'd see him again, if ever. At last, on Monday, 18 December 1989, with very mixed feelings, I boarded a flight from Miami International to Gatwick and then on to Palma in time to spend Christmas with my children.

It was strange getting back. The kids were so much older. Patrick didn't know who I was. It was upsetting. I was euphoric at first but it only lasted two days, maybe not even that long, because I realised pretty quickly how screwed-up the kids were.

They'd had a great time with my oldest sister. She came over with her two little boys and they were always out doing things – going to the beach, sailing. So that was good. But even though they were with her nine months before I came home, they were still very disturbed by what had happened to them before. I tried to talk to them about it, and I'd find little notes and poems they'd written to me, giving some insight into the horror they'd lived through at the hands of my younger sister's boyfriend.

Seeing your parents arrested like that and then being placed in the care of your aunt and her violent boyfriend definitely affected them. Patrick was three when I came back and still not speaking – a child psychologist diagnosed severe trauma. I think there's still a lot of anger there in all of them, particularly the girls. And as I'm the mother I think it is subconsciously directed at me. Mothers are the ones who are meant to be there to nourish and nurture their children. And I wasn't there.

Meanwhile Howard is up there on a pedestal and can do no wrong. While he was in jail he wrote to Amber and said he had done it all for them. How do you figure that one out, or is it that he was trying to convince himself?

Also, we faced horrendous money problems after my return from prison, absolutely horrendous. All my money had gone on keeping the children and paying lawyers' fees and Howard certainly didn't have any. He's always blown money just as fast as he's made it. The only reason we ever had a house was because I'd insist on it. Otherwise he'd have had us all living in five-star hotel rooms and buying up the latest electronic gadgets and toys. The money went on nothing really.

Financially it was a complete nightmare. The first thing I did was sell an apartment we had in Palma Nova. I practically gave it away to raise money to get my sister and her kids back to the States and her husband. I was left with just enough to keep the rest of us going for a year, living frugally. During that time I did up the top floor of the house and rented it out in the summer and just did all sorts of odd jobs. I sometimes look back and think how the fuck did I do it. I still managed to pay their school fees. Just.

All our clothes were donated by friends. I had this friend who used to fly out from England twice a year with M&S bags full of clothes. She was an angel. It was so nice to see the children in new clothes instead of their friends' cast-offs.

I had all sorts of odd jobs. One summer I was working flat out all day. There was this film company and I used to do a lot of the ironing for them. Other friends ran a bar and I was the bouncer, which was a bit bizarre, and I also used to work on the boats. All the jobs I took I only accepted if it meant I could be there when the children came home from school.

And all the time I was worrying about Howard and

about what kind of sentence he'd get. The case against him was stacking up.

After my brother Patrick got only three years, the prosecution immediately said they were going to appeal the sentence under the new laws – in which case Patrick would be facing 125 years or one of those stupidly meaningless American sentences. They threatened him with all sorts of things, which they would have carried out, which is when Patrick agreed to make a statement against Howard. He didn't have any choice. He was either going to spend the rest of his life in jail and leave his children without a dad, or grass Howard up. And let's face it, he wouldn't even have been in there in the first place if it wasn't for Howard sending Moynihan over despite knowing he was working for the DEA. At first I was a bit pissed off with Patrick for testifying against Howard, because Howard had manipulated me to be pissed off. But when you think about it really, he didn't have any choice.

When he first got to the States, Howard said he was going to defend himself but I persuaded him he really needed a lawyer. He was in America now. Then he kept insisting he wasn't going to plea-bargain, he would go to trial. I'm convinced that if he had gone to trial he would have been found guilty and he would never have got out. They would have buried him alive. They'd have put him somewhere like Marion where prisoners are kept underground.

Finally Howard accepted that with Patrick, Ernie and all the other defendants except me testifying against him there was no way he could risk going to trial, so he ended up plea-bargaining. He could have received a sentence up to forty years, but the judge ended up giving him twenty-five. It sounded horrendous, but I knew he would be eligible for parole, so for me it was a bit of a relief because I could see it wasn't going to be for ever, for ever, for ever. It was a fixed sentence and then there were appeals and in fact, as it turned out, the judge lowered his sentence at the appeal and Howard ended up getting parole after seven years. I always felt it wouldn't be as long as it could have been. Sometimes you just know that sort of thing.

The judge in his sentencing said Howard should be sent to a jail with a good psychiatric unit. He obviously thought Howard was mentally unsound. I thought he was mistaken at the time but I agree with him now. To have carried on dealing when you've seen how much evidence they've got against you is completely bizarre.

The worst thing was that, because of my criminal record, I couldn't visit Howard during the seven years he was in prison. I missed him terribly. It's very hard bringing kids up completely on your own. It's hard enough if you're separated but at least you have a part-ner coming round every now and then or sharing the joy of the kids' achievements. It's very demoralising when you haven't got that at all.

Though I spoke on the phone to Howard all the time, I never really had long enough to talk to him properly. The kids were always clamouring to speak to him, and there wasn't enough time.

In fact I was very forgiving, very supportive. I didn't feel resentful at all. I worried about Howard greatly and missed him so much. I'd do petitions, all the time working to get him out in one way or another. Meanwhile he found ways to make prison bearable, as Howard did. He used all his charm. Got a good job teaching, playing tennis. I think he did what he needed to get through.

And then, in April 1995, he came home.

You'd think most people who'd put their family through what we had all gone through would come home and put their heads down and try to make amends, but Howard's attitude was more 'I've suffered seven years in jail. Now I'm going to have fun'. It was as though he was oblivious to what the children and I had gone through.

Money was still a problem so as soon as he came out, I got in touch with the *News of the World*. They flew out to Palma and did an interview with us about him returning home from prison. They paid us £15,000. Immediately there was more money than we'd had in God knows how long. Howard naturally wanted to blow the lot on a holiday. And sulked when I said it wasn't sensible, as we had to figure out how we were going to make a regular living.

I tried to make Howard promise to go straight and he said: 'Of course.' He did take a job teaching as a private tutor for a while in GCSE and A level maths and physics. I continued working at the bar a couple of nights a week and carried on with some guardianship work I had. Then Howard got a £100,000 book deal, to be paid in three instalments and life was a good deal easier.

It was fantastic having him back at first but he soon became very resentful. If Amber or Golly wanted to go out at night, they'd ask my permission because they'd been used to it. I could see he hated that. There were many things he resented. It wasn't that he said anything, one would just feel it.

His life got busier. Newspapers asked him to do book reviews and he had a regular reviewing position with the *FT*, which is a privileged slot to be given. Even so, if he was busy he would have Amber write them. She's bright and a good writer and she did it conscientiously but she was just seventeen. I said: 'You must never let them know that's what you're doing.' But Howard being Howard, with his boundless egotism, thought he could get away with anything. He told them: 'I didn't have time to write this one so I got my daughter to do it.' Naturally the *FT* never commissioned him to do another one. I said, 'Why can't you see things like that annoy people?'

When he finished writing the book and it was published in 1996/7 he was off again. The book instantly became a best-seller. And fame had arrived.

We would watch interviews with him on the television, when he would say he had no regrets about his life and would do it all again. It really was as if he had no idea of the awful suffering we had endured, or he just didn't care. I would see tears welling in Francesca's eyes as she watched.

He started going off on promotional tours and taking class A drugs. I was so shocked when I first realised Howard had taken cocaine. It went against everything he'd always believed. In pre-prison days he wouldn't have it in the house or let anyone around him have it. When I confronted him, he said, 'Why not?' I said, 'It goes against everything you've ever said.' He said, 'Oh, I was stupid.' Then he got into the whole E thing. It was all so different from before he went to prison. I hated it.

While he was off being celebrated, I was still at home in Palma looking after the kids as I'd always done. When Francesca finished her O Levels and before starting her A Levels I suggested to Howard that as he was spending so much time in the UK, we should all move back there. He said he couldn't bear the thought of living back in the UK and as soon as the promotion of the book was finished he wanted to be in Palma to write his next book. *Dope Stories* was written here.

Howard genuinely enjoyed the adulation he was getting and embraced it wholeheartedly. I was happy to see him enjoying his new celebrity life and when I was in the UK with him it amused me to watch him with his fans, although the children and I did on occasions get irritated at how we got shoved out of the way, trampled upon and pushed to the side by people eager to get to him. It annoyed us that he wouldn't do anything to stop that from happening.

We eventually split up in 2003 because I found out that Howard was having a full-on affair that had apparently been going on for about two years. Of course I'd been bloody suspicious about what was going on before that as he was spending so much time away, but he'd always denied it.

I found out first from Patrick, who was sixteen by this time. He'd seen a text. He said, 'Mum, I think you'd better know about this.' It was from someone called Caroline. I said: 'Howard, who's Caroline?' He said: 'I don't know anyone by that name.'

A few months later I managed to break into his emails, as you do. But it's not always the best thing for you to do in the long term. It was pretty awful. I found out a lot more than was good for me, like that she had visited him out here and that he'd even driven her around in the family car.

After everything we'd gone through, to have him do this felt like a complete betrayal. I felt like I'd been completely stabbed in the back.

Of course he was devastated that I had found out. How convenient it was for him having me in Palma, while he played the field in the UK. He could still keep up the pretence of been the 'nice' family man, that he had portrayed in *Mr Nice*.

And then, in 2004, I got breast cancer. Howard came out and stayed with me in hospital while I had the operation in Palma. He left immediately after the operation and to this day I feel I didn't get the emotional support I so needed and feel I was due after all the years of standing by him in prison.

The doctors wanted me to have chemotherapy afterwords. I was pretty shattered, with everything I'd found out about Howard, and wanted a second opinion. I returned to London for a consultation. It was while I was waiting to find out if I needed chemo that Howard slapped the divorce on me. What cruel timing! I felt totally broken and suffered from acute panic attacks.

Sadly, as if Patrick hadn't gone through enough, he was left nursing me through my illness and was heartbroken. I myself was just in pieces. I felt as if I was trapped inside Edvard Munch's painting *The Scream*. Meanwhile Patrick was desperately hoping his father would come home and be the father he had always longed for.

The divorce came through in May 2005. Patrick was still at school and I still needed financial support but I couldn't get through to Howard. I had to bite my tongue a lot.

Writing my own book about my life with Howard was therapeutic, but I had to struggle not to let my anger with him come through. I tried very hard to put myself back into the mindset of how I'd felt at the time and remember how good our life together had been, and how much I'd loved him.

The book came out in 2006, and then the rights were bought by a film company. The film is based on Howard's book with mine as additional source material and is supposed to be coming out in February 2010. The whole family has cameo roles in it.

I haven't seen the film yet and I think it's going to be really weird watching my life being played out in the cinema. Some bits are blatantly untrue, like me being Myfanwy's mother. At least the inaccuracies will help me remind myself it's fiction, not fact.

It's very hard to tell from a script what it will be like. I think it's more the Howard Marks story with me as a supporting actress, than it is about the two of us as equals. But looking back maybe our lives were really like that?

Chloë Sevigny, who plays me, is an amazing actress. And I feel humbled that she is playing me. After the filming finished Chloë remarked to me that she wished she had met me earlier as she would have portrayed me as a lot stronger, which was a nice thing to say but made me slightly worried about how I'll come out in the film.

I hope the film doesn't focus solely on the miserable stuff because my abiding memory of being with Howard is feeling happy. We had a good time, we got on terribly well, we had lovely kids, and we were soulmates as Howard put it. Even now we sometimes get on so well – and then something will happen to remind me of how badly he has behaved.

I still think it's lower than low to do what he did to someone who's shown you so much support, just when they most need support themselves. There are too many things now that I just cannot excuse or forget.

The last few years have been a nightmare. Howard isn't speaking to me at the moment because I told him he was morally corrupt, which he is in many ways, except he doesn't like to be told that. Howard only likes to be told that he's wonderful, and if you criticise him at all he can't stand it. He surrounds himself with people who tell him he's wonderful. It's the egotistic personality always shining through.

In the days we were together, we had nice friends. We met interesting people. These days, the people he has surrounding him tend to be druggies, drunks, villains and hangers-on. He appears on stage shows in small provincial towns, sometimes with Dave Courtney

– a sad testimony to that young boy, with such proud parents, who set off from his small town in Wales to study at Balliol College, Oxford.

Of course I used to think he was wonderful too. Howard had, and continues to have, an amazing ability to make people fall in love with him. When you meet him you get the impression that life with him would never be dull. Howard's charisma wins everyone over, always has and probably always will.

Mr Nice & Mrs Marks *is published by Ebury Press*

'CARLY'

Now twenty-six, Carly [all names in this chapter have been changed] was just eighteen when she became involved with John, a powerful figure fourteen years her senior. John was living on the Costa del Sol after fleeing from his native Ireland where his drug-trafficking activities had earned him the epithet 'Ireland's Most Wanted Man'. Carly, young and naive, was blinded by love and seduced by the opulent lifestyle John was offering. She became so embroiled in John's life and 'work', helping out at every level of the business, that when the relationship began to unravel, she feared he would never allow her to leave. Now a cash-strapped student with a new boyfriend, Carly still hasn't quite left the past behind her. Nervous, but articulate and composed, she checks the door often when giving her interview, and insists all names are changed for fear of reprisals . . .

When I was in college the other day, I took out a pen to copy down some notes. The girl next to me gasped when she noticed the sparkling crystals inset all the way along. I felt my face burn with embarrassment as I returned it quickly to its box. Because that set of two Swarovski pens would probably cost more than that girl lives on in a month. If there was ever a symbol of pointless excess, those jewel-encrusted pens are surely it. They're also one of the few reminders I have left of the life I used to live.

To look at me now, in my nondescript jeans, with my hair scraped back, you'd never believe I used to regularly go out shopping with €3000 or €4000 stuffed into my purse. If I liked a thousand-euro handbag, I'd get three in different colours. I had everything money could buy – Prada, Gucci, Jimmy Choo – the higher the price tag, the more of it I had. And when I grew bored with the boutiques of Marbella and Puerto Banus, I'd fly to New York for the weekend to hit the shops there – first class, of course. I owned a car before I'd had my first driving lesson, and once I passed I drove a different car practically every month – Porsche, BMW – the names were all the same to me. I had everything money could buy. If you could have seen my soul, it probably had a designer label on it. But you know what, I might have gained all this shiny, glittering stuff, but I'd lost something I thought I'd never find again. I'd lost all knowledge of who I was.

I certainly wasn't brought up in that kind of lifestyle. I was born in England and spent my first ten years there in a very normal household. Mum was a nurse, Dad did a variety of different jobs. My brother and I went to school and learned the difference between right and wrong, just like everyone else.

Then, when I was coming to the end of primary school, my parents decided they'd had enough of rising prices and – ironic though it seems now – soaring crime levels in Britain. They decided to move to Marbella on Spain's Costa del Sol, where they believed a better life awaited us.

I went to Spanish school when we moved and got on well, becoming fluent in a very short space of time. We all settled in and though, as a traditional bolthole for UK criminals, it wasn't the promised land it might have seemed, the weather and the beach lifestyle made up for the downsides.

Being fluent in Spanish – not as common as you'd think amongst the notoriously insular British expat community – meant that when I left school I had little trouble finding work. I was offered a job in an upmarket property company specialising in top-end real estate.

One day I was in the office, air conditioning on full to guard against the blazing heat outside, when the door opened. In walked a tall, dark-haired, immaculately dressed man in his early thirties. I was only eighteen, in fact it was my birthday that very day, but even so I realised from the gleaming black car he'd pulled up in, and the gold Rolex watch on his wrist, that here was someone of importance.

He wanted to rent a house, he told me. Somewhere private. As we began talking and I started showing him photographs, I became increasingly aware of how attractive he was, with his soft Irish accent and ready smile. His name was John and, although he was fourteen years older than me, I was young and easily impressed by his clothes and obvious wealth, and flattered by his interest in me.

After that first meeting John went away on holiday, but as soon as he got back he called me up at the office. I was thrilled, particularly when he came to pick me up at my parents' house in a sleek sports car before whisking me off for champagne cocktails. I felt like I'd been plucked from obscurity and straight onto the set of a movie. This was what being adult was all about and I loved it.

I was so smitten with John that when he asked me to move in with him on our third date, I didn't hesitate. At that time I didn't know what he did. I hadn't asked him. Growing up on the Costa del Sol, you learn never to question people too closely about how they make their money.

Of course I knew there was something not quite right about him. From the beginning it was obvious he didn't go out to work from nine to five every day. He seemed to spend most of the day at home, then he'd come to pick me up from work and we'd go out, but there would be telephones ringing all the time, and he'd keep going off into corners to talk to people. I knew that often he'd go out somewhere after dropping me off.

But I was so young, I didn't really care about what he did. I was more interested in the lifestyle he enjoyed and the astonishing fact that someone like him could be interested in me. Of course, now I know that what he saw in me was someone naive enough to be moulded into whatever he wanted and young enough for her loyalty to be bought, but at the time I thought his attention meant I was somehow sophisticated and glamorous.

I gave up work when I moved in with John. It was his idea, but I didn't put up much of a struggle. At eighteen, when you're given a choice between getting up at seven to go to work and staying in bed before spending the day shopping or having lunch, there's really not much contest. I didn't see it as giving up my independence – he said he wanted us to spend more time together and he had plenty of money, so why not?

It wasn't long before the subject of how he made his living came up and I discovered he was a drug smuggler, although I didn't realise at first how big-time he was. I'm ashamed to say it now, but I didn't really think that much of it when he told me. By that stage I was so in love with the guy I'd have overlooked anything. I'd never experienced anything like that before. Coming from such an ordinary family, he seemed so exciting, I was able to push everything else to the back of my mind.

I never really agreed with drugs, but I could justify what he did by reasoning that if he didn't do it, someone else would. He always told me that he didn't create the demand, he just supplied it.

I was completely swept away by him. I'd never been with anyone before who jetted off to New York for the weekend, and flew first class and kept champagne stacked in the fridge like it was bottled water. I was wilfully blind to what it all meant and where it all came from.

The first months together passed in a whirl of shopping and partying. I was just living in the moment. I was so in love, I didn't really see or care what was going on around me. The sheer excess was dizzying. Every three weeks we'd fly off somewhere for the weekend to go shopping, usually New York. And we'd go on fantastic holidays to places I'd never even heard of. One day, he told me he had a surprise for me and took me outside and there was a brand new Mini Cooper sitting in the drive. I hadn't even passed my test!

But it wasn't just about the money – in fact in many ways I preferred him when he was in one of his 'down' periods and we'd stay in, just the two of us, and he could be himself. But he was insecure, and that made him flash his money around. It took me a long time to realise that his way of winning friends and relationships was to buy them. In fact, after we split up he'd say 'but I took you on fantastic holidays' as if you can measure love by how much you spend on someone.

But all that was in the future. In the beginning I was won over by the whole package of him. And part of that package was the drugs thing. I'd love to say I tried to stay out of that side of his life, but I didn't. I became involved in his world bit by bit until I was in it right up to my neck. I didn't even think about it.

It started because he used to stash drugs and money in the house. I'd find cash hidden in the wardrobes, in the car, even in my boots. After a while, that starts to become normal. I think because I was so young, he trusted me. He knew I would basically do what he told me, without asking too many difficult questions. And me speaking fluent Spanish was another major advantage. He started taking me into meetings with him so that I could translate. I'd sit there talking about times and shipments and hundreds of thousands of euros, without even blinking. Before long, he was sending me to meetings on my own, to talk on his behalf. I was so blind I thought that was something to be proud of. I felt pleased that I was contributing something. John paid for everything, so it was my way of giving him something back.

Other evenings, he'd ask me to count cash for him. I'd sit in a locked bedroom surrounded by bundles of notes, steadily counting hundreds and thousands of euros as though they were small change. I didn't get a buzz from it. It just felt normal – something I did to help out, like you'd help out behind the counter if your man was a shopkeeper.

The problem was that John's livelihood made it very difficult for us to have friends. He didn't trust anyone anyway, so he had no close friends, only people he knew through 'work'. And as I wasn't allowed to give people my number or have friends back to the house because he was so paranoid about people knowing where he was, I gradually became alienated from most of the people I knew.

We'd still go to see my parents, and John would be so charming they'd always be reassured that I was having a wonderful time. When they asked what work we both did, we said 'property'. That was our explanation for everything, even though we didn't know the first thing about it. He showered them with expensive presents and took them out to the best restaurants – I wasn't the only one who turned out to be easily bought. But to give them their due, they thought I was happy. And so did I to start with.

The changes happened so gradually, I hardly even noticed them. It made sense at first that I hardly saw my friends. John was convinced the house and the phones were tapped, even the mobiles, so I wasn't allowed to talk to anybody unless I used a payphone.

And they certainly couldn't have my address or number.

I was also a bit embarrassed. My friends knew me and my situation. They'd have taken one look at my house and my new designer wardrobe and they'd have known something wasn't quite right. I didn't want anyone disapproving of me.

My sense of alienation got even more pronounced after John fell out with one of his so-called 'partners'. I found out about the disagreement in dramatic style. We'd gone out to get the Sunday papers. I'd nipped into the shop, still in my slippers, while he waited outside in the car. When I came out, there was this big brawl going on in the street with lots of cars pulling up. Then this guy who John had had a falling out with suddenly appeared, pulled out a gun and pressed it to John's head. I could see his hand shaking. Funnily enough, I'm now quite good friends with this guy, but at the time he was furious and I was terrified.

I started screaming at him, 'What the hell are you doing?', and as he turned to me, John took the opportunity to jump in the car and tear off. It took me a few seconds to fully comprehend that he'd just left me there on my own. This other guy just looked at me – a really awful look. Then he drove off too. I was left standing in the street in my slippers, clutching the newspapers, my mouth hanging open. I didn't know whether this guy had gone off to kill John, I didn't know how I was going to get home. In the end, I rang my dad and said,

'Dad, there's been a bit of an argument.' He said, 'Don't worry, John already phoned me. I'm on my way.' He picked me up and dropped me off at the house. By the time I got in and found John sitting on the sofa, I was fuming. 'Thanks a lot for leaving me,' I spat at him.

After that we had to leave the coast for a bit. It turned out John and this guy had done a drugs deal where he felt John had ripped him off by a few hundred thousand euros. Marbella wasn't safe for us, so we went inland for a few months. I quite enjoyed that period. It was just the two of us, and we couldn't go out much or spend much because we had to keep a low profile, so it was a really quiet, almost peaceful time.

But inevitably we drifted back to the coast, and John got back to 'work'. Again, I quickly became embroiled in his deals. Sitting talking to gangsters about quantities and shipments became second nature. I used to joke to John that if we ever split up I could be a great drug dealer in my own right. I had all the contacts and I knew everything about that world.

I didn't really think about being caught. It sounds crazy but I never thought it could happen to me. John always told me: 'If you get caught, say "no comment, no comment", and they'll let you go.'

I did all sorts of things for John. I was the only one he trusted so I became his right-hand man. I carried money for him, stuffed in my boots. I was one of a convoy of cars that used to go out scouting for police before big meetings or drop-offs. The two of us regularly debugged our house from top to bottom – we'd get bug detectors and go through room by room – I'd do the bedroom and the bathroom, he'd do the living room and the kitchen. We were a team.

It sounds so far-fetched now, but at the time it seemed normal. Don't forget, my whole adult life started with John, so I didn't know anything else. If he said 'can you ring so and so, I need to get some money off them', I'd say 'no problem' and I'd do it.

I was just so young and so won over by the lifestyle that I never really thought about the moral aspects of it. John and I never touched drugs, John hardly even drank and didn't even smoke cigarettes, so it was easy to separate off that side of things. To me it seemed so straightforward. For half an hour's work you get some- thing like 300,000 euros. Why would you do anything else?

Even if we only worked now and then, given that type of return we were still very well off. John had a separate bank account from me, and I never knew how much money he had, but I knew he was worth quite a few million.

The money just didn't seem real to me, once there were that many noughts on it. To me, it was just a way to fund the lifestyle I'd become used to. I'd say 'I need some new trainers for the gym', and there was never any question. I got that first Mini before I even passed my test, and it just sat in the garage gathering dust. When I did get my licence, there were different cars there all the time. I'd drive a Porsche one week and an XR5 the next. We'd go into BMW and they'd treat us like royalty. They all knew us. We'd buy two cars at once. We'd order them straight from the factory and pay a rate every week so that it looked like a 'normal' purchase and we didn't have to do any big transfers.

There were times we had so much money we were moving house every few months just for the hell of it – we wanted an infinity pool, a tennis court, this and that. The last villa had a gym upstairs and if John was working out in it, I'd have to phone him to call him down for dinner, the house was that big.

Looking back, our spending was out of control. We'd walk past a showroom window and I'd say, 'I quite like that Golf', and he'd just go in and buy it for me. Or he'd say, 'Do you want a watch? What kind of watch do you want?' I'd say, 'I don't know. Any watch.' Now I've got a Tag, I've got a Cartier, I've got a Rolex.

Or I'd say, 'Oh, look at those lovely Louis Vuitton bags', and it would be: 'What colour do you want? Why don't you get it in all the colours?' Then the next minute it was a Jimmy Choo bag I was after.

Though I didn't notice at the time, John was very controlling. That's obviously why he picked someone so much younger than him – he knew he could shape me into the person he wanted me to be.

Even when we went out shopping for clothes, he'd try to manipulate me. We'd walk in somewhere and I'd ask him if he liked something and he'd say, 'Not really'. Then I'd put it back. I desperately wanted his approval.

I wasn't afraid of him because I never did anything to upset him. There were never arguments because I did everything to please him.

As the years went on, our domestic situation became increasingly unhealthy. It was just me and him. He didn't trust anyone so he didn't really have any friends. We were together 24/7. We ran out of conversation. We ran out of everything. I lost myself completely. I simply didn't know who I was any more. But it's only now that I can see how destructive the situation was.

While John would buy me anything I wanted and lavish presents on me, I never had any money of my own. He either paid for things, or else doled out the money when I needed it. It was his way of keeping me in place.

We almost got married one time. I was going on and on and on about wanting to be engaged. I don't know why I was so obsessed. I suppose it was about insecurity, or maybe I just thought that's what you were supposed to do. Eventually he said, 'Do you want to get married?' I said 'yes' and he told me to go out and get a ring, and handed me a wad of money. I went out and got myself a ring. I've still got it. But as soon as I'd bought it, I realised it wasn't the ring I wanted after all, it was the togetherness. Without that, it was meaningless.

John had a child who lived with her mother back in Ireland. He used to get me to fly over to fetch her because he was on the run for drug trafficking and if he'd tried to enter the country he'd have been arrested and locked away for twenty years or something.

I vaguely knew about it, but still it was a shock when the Sunday paper one day carried a photo of me with John, plus a few pictures of our house and the caption 'Ireland's Most Wanted Man'.

My parents saw it and of course they were concerned about me, but there was only so much they could say. At that stage I was too entrenched to imagine life without him. I just told them not to worry.

But our reclusive lifestyle was taking its toll. Being together all the time created this unhealthy little world that became increasingly cut off from normality. John was obsessed with the house being clean – which he saw as my responsibility. He was really controlling about that. He'd walk round running a fingertip over the surfaces to see if they were dirty. He'd ask, 'Why isn't my T-shirt ironed? What else have you got to do?' Nowadays I'd tell him to eff off, but by that stage I was like a robot. I did exactly what he said.

It was so ironic. Materially, I had everything I wanted, but I felt I'd lost all control over my life. The only area I could still control was my weight – so I started obsessively exercising and dieting, becoming skinnier and skinner.

I'd get up in the morning around five and head straight to our indoor gym to exercise. Then I'd take the dogs out – we had two bull mastiffs. When I came back, I'd start cleaning the house. Then it would be around nine o'clock and I'd start getting John's breakfast ready. He'd get up around ten and I'd give him his breakfast, then I'd clear away and go back to the gym where he might join me. After we'd washed and changed we'd go out to make phone calls and go shopping. We might go to Starbucks, or out for lunch or whatever, followed by more shopping and a movie. Or we'd come home and have dinner and lay on the sofa and watch the television. I'd take a bath and go to bed. Of course, that all changed if there was work on. If there was work, we'd do that instead of going into town.

The few friends I'd managed to hold on to were worried about me because I got so thin. At one point I weighed fifty kilos. I didn't notice it. I thought I was fat. I worked out obsessively hour after hour. Every spare moment I would be in that gym. It was a mixture of frustration, depression and unhappiness. It was my way of taking control over at least one part of my life.

After we'd been together four or five years, I started admitting to myself that things had become unbearable. It doesn't matter how many amazing holidays you have if you can't tell anyone about them because no one's allowed to have your number. It doesn't matter how many flash meals you eat if you go to bed afterwards wondering if this is the night the police come and kick down the door. Every time John went out at night, I'd be worried sick yet I had no way of getting in touch with him to find out where he was.

The lowest point came when I became pregnant. I was only young but I still didn't want to have an abortion, yet John was adamant I couldn't go ahead with the pregnancy. Because of his 'work', he'd already had to leave one child behind when he fled, and now he hardly saw her. He wasn't prepared to go through all that again. He said to me, 'One way or another, you're not going to have this child.' I didn't know what he meant, but I didn't want to find out. I felt it was all wrong that he was the one making the decision, but I didn't have the courage to say no to him.

So I had to travel back to England to have an abortion, even though it wasn't what I wanted to do. Again, because he was a wanted man, he couldn't come with me so I had to go on my own. I couldn't tell my parents because I was too ashamed.

It was a horrible experience and afterwards I suffered a lot of depression as a result. I had to see a psychiatrist and go on medication. I even thought about committing suicide. John grew impatient. He'd say, 'Well, just stop thinking about it.' I'd say, 'Sorry, but I just can't stop thinking about it. It plays on my mind every single day of my life.' Even now, not a day goes by when I don't think about it. I think some women can put things like that behind them, but the fact that it wasn't through my own choice still gets to me. I did it because I thought it was the right thing to do, but I regretted it straight away. I can't even begin to describe the amount of tears I cried over that lost baby. I was so lost after that. I was stuck in the house, stuck in the relationship, stuck in this weird world that wasn't real.

By this time John and I had moved into separate bedrooms. We were like prison-mates, we weren't even friends.

My life became hell, but I didn't know how to get out of the situation. I was afraid that because John had put so much trust in me, and because of the things I'd seen and done and witnessed, and the stories I'd heard, he wouldn't be able to let me go.

He'd invested so much in me – both in terms of money and time and energy. He'd moulded me into this person he needed. And because he was so much older than me, I'd done exactly what he told me to do. I'd been completely blind. I'd given him everything – heart, soul, the lot. But in return all I'd had was things: a fantastic holiday, a new bag.

Everything seemed to be spiralling out of my control. One time I was out driving with John and two cars rammed into the side of ours then drove off. Then I got mugged one Valentine's Day by people he had obviously been involved with. They rammed my car, came in and took everything from me – money, bag, the lot. I was terrified but I couldn't go to the police and report it because I couldn't give away any details. There could never be anything linking us to the house or me to him.

I knew I had to try to get away before I lost myself completely. I started to build bridges with old friends and go out a lot more. John didn't like it, but I just did it anyway. I stopped spending so much time cleaning the house. John's laundry wasn't done. I didn't make his breakfast. That was the first step towards breaking the control he had over me.

I confided in an old friend about how unhappy I was and asked her what I should do. She said, 'Well, you've got to get back to work.' But the problem was I couldn't apply for a job without giving details – phone numbers, address. And I couldn't give away any of that because it could lead the authorities to John.

I was in a catch-22. I needed money to leave, but I couldn't get any without jeopardising everything. The thought of leaving without any money scared me to death. I was so used to a certain lifestyle by that stage. I was used to walking into Prada or Gucci or Louis Vuitton and getting what I wanted. If I said, 'I want to go shopping', I'd get two or three grand put in my hand. Or I'd say, 'Let's go to Las Vegas for the weekend', and he'd say, 'OK, we'll stop off in New York on the way to do some shopping.'

John had always drilled into me that after getting used to that kind of life, I'd never be able to go back to 'normality'. For my part, I dreamed of a 'normal' life, but no longer really knew what that was.

I planned my getaway so many times over the weeks and months. In my mind, I left him over and over again, but I always went back. Of course he didn't know I'd even gone, but I had. I'd get my dogs and I'd get in my car. Then I'd turn around because I thought: if he finds me, he'll kill me.

In reality, I didn't actually know what he'd do. I'd seen him in a bad mood and it was frightening, but he'd never been physically violent towards me. His scare tactics were always psychological. He knew my weaknesses and I worried that he'd use them against me.

In a lot of ways pity as well as fear kept me from leaving. John didn't have friends, his family hardly ever came to visit. If I left him he'd be totally on his own. I worried how he'd cope. You can't spend six years with someone without caring a bit about what happens to them.

But I knew I had to get out of there for my own sanity. One day, after a particularly tense evening the night before, I rang my friend and said, 'I've had enough. I'm going to do it.' My friend told me not to do anything hasty, but to come round and talk. When I got there he said, 'Why don't you apply for a job at the company where I work?' He had some forms there and helped me fill them in, using his number and address. I did, and within days, I had an interview to be a personal assistant to one of the directors.

That's when I broke the news to John. I was really scared of telling him and rehearsed over and over again what I would say. I had no idea how he'd react, but to my surprise, he was all right. I think he'd seen I was slipping away but, to be honest, I think he'd also reached such a state of misery with the relationship that he knew something had to be done. He could have stopped me if he wanted – he had so much control over me – but I think he'd given up wanting to. He said, 'If that's what you want to do, that's your right. The door's always open for you here.'

I couldn't actually believe he was going to make it that easy for me, but he did. I moved back home to my parents' house for a bit and got the PA job which at least gave a structure to my life. Gradually I started making inroads back into the real world, the world of normal people. It was such a relief.

When I decided to go back to college to qualify as a translator, John offered to pay for my course. At first I wasn't keen because I didn't want to get back into a situation where I felt indebted to him, or to feel that he had any control over my life. Then I thought about it properly and decided he owed me. I gave him six years of my life and went to hell and back and walked away with nothing except a few designer bags and watches. Besides, it wasn't as if he couldn't afford it.

I still get on OK with John. We have a good relationship, if you can have a good relationship with an ex. I've got a lot more confidence with him now than when we were actually together. I can talk back to him, and I can tease him which I never did before.

Of course I don't have a telephone number for him, so I have to wait for him to get in touch with me. But when he does we're always amicable. Despite everything, I still have a lot of affection for him and I worry about him. I feel sorry for him actually. He has no life. He doesn't dare let anyone else get close to him. He stayed with me because he trusted me, but now I've gone he has no one.

If two weeks or three weeks pass without hearing from him, I worry whether he's OK. I certainly don't want anything bad to happen to him, even though never a day goes by when I don't think how glad I am to be away from him.

Sometimes John talks about giving the whole thing up. Every time he does a deal, or something goes wrong, he says it's the last time but it never is. He earns more money per hour through drugs smuggling than he ever could doing anything else. But the ironic thing is that he's got all this money, but no life.

When I ask him what he's been up to, he says, 'Oh, I've been to the gym. Doing this, doing that.' He's too careful to mention anything about work. Now, I can't imagine I ever lived like that. And I would never ever go back to that kind of life again. Even if someone said to me, 'Don't worry, you'll never ever get caught', I would never go back to that. No way.

Sometimes I worry about how much I know. But I think John and his business partners know I'd never give away any details of what I learned. Anyway, most of the drug dealers and smugglers I met were quite nice, pleasant people. I haven't got bad things to say about them. That's not to say I approve of what they're doing, but I'm realistic. If they don't do it, someone else will. It's never going to go away.

I thought John might make trouble when I started seeing my new boyfriend, who's a paramedic, but he says he's happy for me. He realises now that he did cause me a lot of mental problems and I think in his way he's sorry about it.

I do still have issues over certain things. I'll get in a state if the cleaning's not done and my new partner will say, 'What on earth is wrong with you? It's not the end of the world if the vacuuming doesn't get done.'

I haven't told my new partner much about John. I just tell him it's water under the bridge – but he's picked up some details. He knows he was very rich, and that makes him feel inadequate sometimes, but I love the normality of my life now. If I want something, I have to save up for it, like everyone else. We go shopping at Lidl, eat at McDonald's. I used to have a wardrobe full of Manolos. Now when I go out shopping it's an £8 bag in Primark.

The novelty of having a partner who works a normal job for a normal monthly wage won't ever wear off. I used to dream of being with someone who loved me for me, not because I was of some use to him. I'm sure that's why John stayed with me after things went so badly wrong between us – because I was useful to him and helped him with work. That's not how a relationship should be.

Nowadays, when I look back on my life with John, it's like seeing a book or a film and I have to remind myself that I was that person. I was there. It doesn't seem real. It was me sitting down with that major Colombian drug dealer. It was me negotiating on John's behalf. It's all so difficult to believe now. If I was to try to describe it to any of my friends, they'd think it was all bullshit because it's so far-fetched.

Sometimes I have to get out one of my €2000 watches, just to prove it really did happen to me. I've kept them all. The thing is, I know they're real, but everyone else just thinks they're fake. I go into college with my Jimmy Choo bag and no one knows it costs thousands. The crucifix I wear is Tiffany. Someone said to me the other day, 'I didn't know you were religious,' and I said, 'I'm not, but it's Tiffany and I love it.' They said, 'What's Tiffany?' It makes me laugh. I've got my pens I use for my course and they're set with crystals by Swarovski.

And when I go into the budget supermarket to do the shopping, I carry my purse in a €3000 bag.

By the end, it wasn't hard to give up that lifestyle though. The only thing I miss is my lovely trips to New York. Now if I travel, I've got to sit in economy. Of course I'd rather go first class, but I'd never go back to the life I had. I did live the high life but in the end the lows overtake the highs. There are no mediums. You're either up there, or down here.

That's not to say I regret it. It was a real learning experience. If I hadn't gone through all of that, I wouldn't be who I am. In many ways it has made me a lot more mature. I listen to some of the kids at college talking about what drugs they had at the weekend, where they got them from. And I'm thinking: yep, I know that guy. I feel worlds apart from any of them.

It makes me laugh when I see films or read books glamorising the kind of life I used to have. Girls get sucked into this idea that it's so exciting – shopping all day, buying stuff. But do you know what? I had no conversation by the end. I had all the flashy clothes in the world, but all I did was stay in and talk about work, or *EastEnders*.

I've got a good friend who's dying to get her hands on a millionaire. She thinks it's all about staying at the Savoy and wearing fantastic clothes. I say to her, 'Listen, it's not all it appears. You're being bought, and it's really not worth it.' But she won't listen.

Walking around Marbella and Puerto Banus, I see women in the position I used to be in, and they've got these flash clothes and they're driving around in these flash cars, and I think: been there, done that. Not impressed. I'm so glad I'm finished with all that.

It's almost as if I've lived my life backwards. People usually wait all their lives to accumulate a few lovely things. I've got all the lovely things I want, and now I'm happy to go back to the basics. I've done so much more than most people do in their whole lives. In some ways I'm glad I did it all. I've done that now. I know what it's like. Now I can get on with my life.

Now I just want to work for a few years and earn my own money. Before I started college, I used to love getting my wage slip at the end of the month, knowing it was money I'd worked for. In a weird way, I even love having the stress of having no money because I feel normal.

I love not being able to go out and eat all the time. I love going home and cooking a dinner and sharing a bottle of wine. I love the normality of it all. I love making sure everything is turned off so we don't use too much electricity. I find it fun because I had so many years of not caring about all that, which actually just made me isolated and cut off from how most people were living their lives.

When my current boyfriend apologises because he can't buy me a flash present for my birthday, I tell him not to be sorry. I'm glad he doesn't have money because it means we're both working towards something together. Because I've had the alternative and it got me nothing in the end – just a Gucci bag, some Manolo shoes and a lot of heartache.

I'd really like other women to know the truth about the real lives behind these men. You see films and television glamorising criminals and it's so not glamorous. It's the opposite. Yeah, there's the bags and the shoes. But all the bags and shoes in the world can't make up for living a life where you can't have friends and you're stuck together day in, day out with someone you're sick of, and you lose sight of who you are.

I spent years being depressed, and floundering around trying to remember the person I'd once been. There I'd be in my seven-bedroomed house with my swimming pool and my gym and my dressing room full of clothes. But I'd lost who I was. Only now am I finally starting to rediscover myself again.

JACKIE 'LEGS' ROBINSON

Should terrorists be classed as gangsters? Clearly that's debatable. But Johnny 'Mad Dog' Adair, former skinhead and one-time loyalist commander, was linked to so many other criminal activities – drug dealing, extortion, as well as murder – that he warrants inclusion. Johnny Adair started out a loyalist hero. When he was jailed for sixteen years in 1994 for directing terrorism, he achieved cult status, but his bloodthirstiness and greed for power when he was released five years later under the Good Friday agreement, led to him becoming Enemy Number One among Protestants and Catholics alike. He was returned to jail in 2002 to serve the rest of his sentence, and fled to England and then Scotland for his own safety following his eventual release in 2005.

Although Johnny was married to wife Gina, he had a very public eight-year affair with Jackie 'Legs' Robinson (so called because of her penchant for short skirts which showed off her long legs). Jackie fell in love with him almost against her own better judgement, and stuck by him despite the killings, the excessive drug taking, and the stress of finding herself involved in a three-way tug-of-love that she was never going to win.

Now fifty-two, Jackie still lives in Belfast, although the city is very different to how it was at the height of the Troubles, when Johnny ruled the roost. Nowadays, she tries to keep a low profile and distance herself from her disgraced former lover, although as she says, people have long memories there. Clearly still conflicted about her feelings for him, she talks almost in the same breath both of closing the door on the past and of the possibility of seeing him again one day. But she knows any reunion would take a lot of setting up as Johnny now lives in exile in Scotland, having made too many enemies ever to set foot back in Northern Ireland.

I never even looked at Johnny Adair at first. I thought he was a little wee fat thing. I was embarrassed by him, in fact. We were in the Taughmonagh Social Club when I first set eyes on him and he said to my friend: 'Tell her I want her.' Well, I thought he was a laughing stock.

The truth was I'd only just moved back to Belfast from England when I first met Johnny Adair. I'd had a bit of a transformation physically since the breakdown of my marriage. Within the space of a few months I'd gone from looking drab to bloody good, and everyone was after me.

I'm quite shy and I didn't respond to Johnny. Women usually threw themselves at his feet because of his status and power so he was intrigued by me, I think. The fact was, I didn't know who he was, although I later heard he was a loyalist commander.

The girls he'd been with before would want to be looked after. I'm a strong-minded person. I can look after myself. I think he recognised that from the beginning and liked it.

After that first meeting I kept seeing him around and he kind of grew on me. A few weeks down the line, I went home and couldn't get him out of my head. Earlier that night he'd rapped on my car window while I was in the club's car park. It was the first time I'd really seen him up close and I felt I'd seen the person he really was beneath the façade. Normally, as I found out, he never let his guard down, but it was as if he had done that with me and I'd seen something no one else could see.

I had an instinct inside me about him. I started to look forward to seeing him and gradually we got together. One week he brought a drink to the table I was sitting at, set it down and then left again. The next week he came back and we started chatting.

He's not the hard person people think. There's a

softer side to him that other people don't see. That's the side I was attracted to.

I started to fall in love with him. We started to go to parties together. One night, we'd gone to a party and we were sat on the stairs when this absolutely stunning girl came up to us. He'd been going out with her before and he dropped her for me. She bent over and whispered in his ear and I thought he'd go off with her, but instead he looked at me sheepishly, and then we started to kiss and it went from there. We quickly became as much of an item as he was with his girlfriend Gina, who was the mother of his four children.

Johnny says himself that I brought out something inside him – that softer side. He didn't like the women that threw themselves at him. That's not what he wanted. It was him I fell in love with, not the status of who he was.

Sometimes we'd be out and I'd go off to the bar or the toilet and when I came back there'd be one or two women fawning over him, but as soon as he saw me, he'd tell them where to go. I did have some power over him in that way.

It was always a complex three-way affaire because of Gina. The two of them had a very tempestuous relationship and each saw other people. I always accepted that Gina was part of the equation, that he wanted both of us, but I wouldn't accept him seeing anyone else. It was always quite twisted. By the end of the time I was with him, I realised that he needed me so that he'd have something to bounce his relationship with Gina against.

I stood firm with Gina and she knew I wasn't going to take anything from her. It may sound like a strange set-up, but during the Troubles, normal rules didn't really apply. The men lived for the moment at that time. They didn't know if they would be coming home the next day. In actual fact they were often more afraid of their wives than of the Republicans.

The wives used their power to get new furniture and they turned a blind eye to what their men were doing. Most women involved with these men just went along with it and stood by them no matter what. It was just how things were in Northern Ireland.

I had a vague idea what Johnny did at the beginning but it wasn't until a serious attempt was made on his life by the IRA that it sank in what a big fish he was, but by that stage I was already too involved with him to back away.

It probably sounds naive but I never worried about me or my own kids or my home being a target, even though he and his friends were coming and going all the time and we had lots of parties at my house. I didn't realise how dangerous it was for my kids and me. We'd make a joke of checking under the car before driving off.

And I believe he was in love with me. The first time I realised how he felt was when I walked into a bar and he was standing with a group of mates and he said, 'See her, fellas. I fucking love her.'

There's mental disability in Johnny's family. He can't grow up in any way. He's every bit the clown, and plays to an audience. But when he was with me he was a different person. If we were out and he belittled people, I'd make him apologise. I'm not into all that. When he started to intimidate people, I'd make him say sorry. If he ordered someone to get a beating, I'd make him back off. I was the only one who could get him to apologise.

Where Johnny, when he was on show, was all showing off and bravado, I'm not like that. I'm caring and loving and in return I found a loving Johnny who needed to be needed and loved.

I know people find it difficult to understand how anyone could fall in love with someone like Johnny Adair, but he was so different with me. He was addicted to the attention he got from others. When we were out people would fall over themselves to shake his hand, and he got off on it, he was this bullying person; but when we were on our own he completely changed. When he came through my door, he was a different character. He had a very big heart. If he knew someone was in prison for Christmas, he'd make sure that person's wife got money to buy the kids' presents.

I never questioned where the money came from, but I noticed he began carrying big wads of cash. It was obvious to me that there were deals going on – extortion rackets, drug dealing – but we never discussed financial matters.

Because of the situation, I was able to shut off from what he did. Don't forget, as far as any of us were concerned, there was a war going on. You'd see Republicans shooting at innocent people and you'd think it was justified at the time, what Johnny and the others were doing.

But that's not to say I didn't have a tussle of conscience. Just because I went out with a terrorist doesn't mean I don't have a conscience.

I was involved. I used to do things for the UDA like gun-running, but then we were fighting a war. After the Shankill bombing I was so angry I would have planted a bomb if I'd been asked. But because of my association with Johnny I was considered too high-profile at the time.

Johnny is a natural born leader. If it hadn't been the Troubles, something else would have come along to make him into a leader. But at the end of the day, he started as a housebreaker. He was pulled in by the UDA and they threatened to break his legs if he didn't join the youth wing. He started his own unit – C Company – and put the old company out and took charge.

I got on well with the members of C Company. I

never judge anybody – I don't feel I have the right to do that. They were fun-loving and we had a good time together. When you're in the thick of it, you just can't believe that the people you're socialising with are malicious enough to pull a trigger or hack someone to death.

I think Johnny assumed that I knew about his antics, but I didn't. I only knew what I was told second-hand. Most women in my position didn't see their men as being responsible for the shootings, bombings and beatings we saw on the television news. You switch off. How else would you realistically cope?

There were a lot of drugs around at that time and I got into it by accident. My drink was spiked at a party. They gave me white powder which I thought would settle a bad stomach, but it was Ecstasy. It gave me a buzz and after that I did a lot of drugs.

It was very damaging to me at the time, but you know I don't regret a thing. I don't regret my past. It's made me who I am.

Johnny really cared about my opinion. When we were both being interrogated in Castlereagh, in the wake of reprisals over the October 1993 Shankill Road bombings, he was more worried about what the police were telling me about him than anything else. He kept asking: 'Did it make you think worse of me?'

Those five days of interrogation in Castlereagh were a nightmare but I kept denying I even knew Johnny and eventually they let me go. But my children were very affected by the whole thing and I felt incredibly guilty about what I'd put them through.

Johnny was arrested again in 1994 on charges of directing terrorism. At first he was held in the notorious Crum prison – until they staged a riot. One day I was feeling really down thinking about him when a friend rang to tell me to turn on the news, and there was Johnny jumping up and down on the roof of the Crum. I thought it was hilarious.

After that he was transferred to the Maze prison, which was effectively run by the prisoners rather than the authorities. Johnny even got himself a mobile phone in there, though they were quite unusual at the time. We used to smuggle in vodka inside balloons in our knickers. The cubicles in the visiting area were high and it was a given that intimate stuff might be going on. Everyone knew that partners were going to have sex in there

I was in court for his trial in September 1995. I was upset the whole time. He was sentenced to sixteen years. When I heard the verdict, I was dazed. I jumped up in court and yelled: 'I'll wait for you Johnny.'

During his first year in prison, Johnny finished with Gina for a while, but he still phoned her all the time. She manipulated him. I'd get angry with Johnny because of that – he was like a naughty child in my hands.

I was madly in love with him when he and Gina split up, and desperate to have his baby. We got engaged while he was in prison and I had an engagement party to celebrate. I'll never forget that night. Obviously Johnny couldn't be there, but he sent me a present which I unwrapped in front of everyone in the bar – a twelve-inch vibrator with a note saying 'Make sure you wait until the wee man gets out, but use this in the meantime'. But the engagement was broken off within a week.

I don't regret all those ups and downs. It was my life at that time. But I do regret giving him so much support when he was going between Gina and me. I even forgave him after we got engaged and then he went and married Gina.

When he married Gina, it broke my heart. The day of the wedding he rang me and he was laughing. He thought it was a big joke. I said the marriage was doomed.

Gina rang me later. She actually said, 'You're a nice person.' I said, 'Do me a favour. Give him the love he deserves. He's a good man.' It was the only time we called a truce.

After Johnny and Gina got married, he still called me all the time. I regret being his agony aunt and his sex therapist. He'd come off the phone to her and then cry to me about something she'd done.

I knew I shouldn't go near him after they got

married, but it was a case of my mind telling me 'no' and my heart telling me 'yes'. Johnny was like a child in many respects. I couldn't leave him because I had this mother thing about him.

I kept up seeing him in prison and was even granted 'private visits' with Johnny where we could have sex. I desperately wanted his child because I wanted something permanent from him. We did agree to try and did that for six years or so. I don't know whether it was because of the steroids he was taking, but it never happened.

I was all over the place emotionally. I got heavily involved with shoplifting and robberies and credit card fraud. Sometimes I'd steal to buy the things Johnny asked me to get him in prison, like designer clothes, but I can't blame him for that, despite how crazy he made me.

Johnny would ring me all the time from prison, even though he was supposedly married to Gina. I couldn't move on with my life at all. It really messed with my head and I had two mental breakdowns.

By the time Johnny was released early from jail in 1999, he had enemies. He managed to piss a lot of people off by shooting his mouth off and being so changeable. He was too mouthy. He wanted to be known, and when he did get known, he didn't like it. He brought a lot of it on himself.

Even then we carried on seeing each other, despite

everything I'd gone through, until something happened to finally bring me to my senses. He suggested I work as a prostitute in a loyalist-run brothel. It was the final straw. I stuck my fist in his face and broke his nose. After that, he tried to make me think it was a joke, but I knew it wasn't. I decided I wasn't going to let him carry on making a fool out of me.

I knew then that it was never going to work, no matter how much effort I put into it. It was the hardest decision I ever made. I had been such a good influence on him. I told him he was getting too greedy. He used to call me Mystic Meg because everything I predicted came true, but he should have listened to me. I'm convinced that if I'd stayed with him, he'd still be here. He wouldn't have gone as power-mad as he did.

Over the next few years, in and out of prison, Johnny pulled the whole Protestant community apart. He wanted full power of the Shankill and the UDF. You can't do that. Johnny was hated by the UDF.

By the end, Johnny saw himself as King of Ireland. He wanted full control of everything.

I'd always said I'd never turn against Johnny but I felt sick when Gina sold her story to the *Daily Mirror*, saying how she'd stood by him while he was in prison when I was the one who visited him all those years. I read about how Gina was pining away without her love, and how she'd had to endure 3000 nights without

Johnny. In 2002, I told my own story in the *Mirror* to set the record straight.

When I read my story in the paper – 'Johnny Adair's Lover Reveals All' – I got a shock reading my own words. It was only then I realised what I'd been through and what my kids had been through and how crazy it had all been. I turned a corner after that.

When Johnny was released from prison for good in 2005, he had little support left and his friends and family were threatened with death unless they left the Shankill area. If he ever came back to Ireland he'd be shot dead within seconds.

Gina settled in Bolton while Johnny ended up going to live in Scotland. They're not together any more. I still don't think he can handle the fact he's a nobody. Johnny will go anywhere he has support, wherever people will look up to him and make him feel big about himself. He has always been in denial and he'll keep going that way for the rest of his life.

I still miss the good times but Johnny betrayed a lot of people. He turned out to be a loser. He betrayed every one of the people who supported him. He became too greedy. Even so, no one knows the whole truth.

Sure, people have given me a hard time over Johnny. I still live in Belfast and in most people's eyes I'm still Johnny Adair's mistress, even though he's been gone all these years. People get afraid. That fear still exists.

I now have a lot of Catholic friends. Even at the height of the Troubles I had Catholic friends. I wouldn't want to dredge everything up again.

I wish I could leave that part of my life behind. Even after all these years I don't live a normal life here. Everyone knows who I am when I go into a bar. I'm afraid to get involved in conversations in case the subject comes round to him. I don't want to be singled out just because of the man I was once involved with.

I've been called all the names under the sun. The whole focus for people's anger in Ireland has been turned on Johnny Adair.

I would like to see him again. I think about it all the time and he obviously wants to see me. Last year he rang the local journalist to ask for my number. A friend of his sent me a message a few months ago saying Johnny often talks about what would have happened if he hadn't chosen Gina, if he'd made a different decision. There's definitely some unfinished business there. I think maybe I'll go over to the UK where he's living now. There's a need for me to bring closure into my life, and he can't come back here.

I've never settled with anyone else and neither has he. I don't think I'll ever love anyone like I loved him. He gave me so much love and no one else has come close.

I wouldn't go down the road of getting back with him though. I wouldn't want it all to kick off again. I had two mental breakdowns. I can't believe I put myself through it, or put up with it.

It makes me angry sometimes when young kids think he's an icon. He's infamous, but in many ways he's teaching young people the wrong way.

Johnny is an icon, but he's not a hero to me. He's a man – the man I fell in love with.

In Love With a Mad Dog *by June Caldwell and Jackie 'Legs' Robinson is published by Gill & Macmillan*

ANDREA GIOVINO

No gangsters' wives' book would be complete without an account of marrying into the Mafia. Growing up in a large Italian family in 1960s Brooklyn, Andrea Giovino learned from an early age to idolise Mafia guys. As a woman, and a very attractive one at that, she had a succession of relationships with powerful Mafia-connected men including Frank Lino, a 'capo' in the Bonanno crime family and Mark Reiter, an associate of the Gambini family, who is currently serving a 260-year prison sentence for narcotics trafficking. During her time as a 'Mafia wife' she was involved in loan sharking and money laundering. In 1992, she was arrested on drugs charges and decided to turn police informant. John Fogarty, her boyfriend at the time, and her brother Johnny, both guilty of multiple murders, also agreed to cooperate with police in return for her release. After refusing to join the Witness Protection Program, she moved to Pennsylvania with her children where she lived quietly for many years until her autobiography, Divorced from the Mob *(Da Capo*

Press), turned her into an unlikely champion for women involved in relationships with abusive men.

When my book, *Divorced from the Mob* came out in 2004, a lot of people thought I was crazy. After all, my evidence had helped to put a lot of people away and I'd had to flee New York City with my children because of threats to my life. Anyone normal would have hidden away in fear, right?

But I'm not the sort of person to live like that. I don't want to live my life constantly looking over my shoulder. I won't give anyone that kind of power over me. And weirdly, going public has made things better for me. I'm always in the public eye now and ironically, that makes me feel safer.

Where I grew up, cooperating with the police goes against every unwritten rule and value. I grew up in Brooklyn, in a mostly Italian neighbourhood. I was the sixth of ten children and there was never enough money to go round. Some of my earliest memories are of my mother – who dominated the family, including my father – sending me out into the cold early morning, shivering in ragged hand-me-downs, to steal bread, bagels and milk from the trays that had just been delivered and left on the pavement outside the neighbourhood corner store. I would have been about five and I guess my mother decided sending me made sense. After all, who'd want to see a little girl arrested for stealing food for her family.

There was a lot of poverty where we lived. There were too many people crammed together with little or no education. People did anything to feed their families – crimes for survival.

My mother was tough and always trying to think of ways to make money. One of those was setting up an illegal gambling den in our basement. Just after I turned six, groups of men started showing up at our house regularly. I'd know they were there because I'd see this long line of fancy cars out front. Our neighbours must have known these were Mafia guys. I don't know what the financial arrangements were but, as much as money mattered to my mother, she also enjoyed the prestige involved in having mob-related men and activities going on in our house. She'd point to these men as they were leaving and tell me that they were the kind of men I should find when I grew up. And they were exactly the kind of men I did find.

Although my mother had to close down the gambling den when she was arrested, the ambition to marry a mobster never left me. It was the only ambition I knew. For a girl it was assumed I wouldn't bother with an education, I'd just get a boyfriend instead. I grew into an attractive young woman with a nice body and I used that as my ticket to a better life. I had no schooling behind me. The future was frightening. All

I could do was hope to find a well-connected man to support me.

By 1977, I hadn't done too well in that respect. I was a single mother with a failed marriage behind me. My big chance came when I was offered a job serving drinks at another illegal gambling club hidden away in a Brooklyn industrial park. The people in the club were as restrained and refined as any group you'd find in a Manhattan nightspot – with one difference. The vast majority had either killed someone themselves, ordered or witnessed a killing, or knew someone who'd done the killing. I understood all this, but instead of being frightened by it, I was intrigued. Being able to rub elbows with some of the underworld's elite was fuel for my fantasies of acquiring nice things.

That's how I met Frank Lino, one of the captains in the Bonanno crime family and just about the most powerful man I could expect to meet. One day he called one of my brothers in and told him he wanted me to be his girlfriend. My mother was delighted. It was every-thing she'd ever dreamed of. How could I refuse?

While I didn't love Frank, I grew very fond of him. We enjoyed a lavish lifestyle. For the first Valentine's Day we spent together, he bought me a brand new 1978 Mercedes 450SL convertible. My favourite outings with Frank were our shopping trips to Manhattan. He'd have his limo pick us up, and we'd get dropped off at Fifth Avenue, then make our way up toward Central Park.

Frank lavished diamonds, gold and other gems on me and bought us both matching platinum Presidential Rolex watches. He had homes in an exclusive area of Brooklyn called Marine Park and in Florida and a ski home on Hunter Mountain in upstate New York.

He was a man who seemed to have a near limitless supply of cash. I thought nothing of driving around in my Mercedes with thousands of dollars in my purse – at least I had that amount at the beginning of the day.

Frank and I seldom talked about business, but I knew that he was involved in the sale of drugs. The romanticised notion of the old-time mob guys not wanting to be involved in drugs is exactly that – an outdated and inaccurate picture of a far more disturbing reality.

But while I did care for Frank and he was very good to me, I knew that somewhere within him had to be a dead place, otherwise he couldn't have gotten to where he was. And if it was there it could come out some day. I didn't want to be around to witness it, or fall victim to it.

After Frank came other relationships with wealthy men such as Mark Reiter, who was eventually sentenced to 260 years without parole for drug trafficking. I made many mistakes choosing partners. They weren't violent towards me but they tended to be abusive and have no respect for women. To them, a woman's place was in the kitchen or the bedroom.

The truth is, I liked the money and the lifestyle. I liked the thrill of socialising with people like John Gotti. It's very glamorous when you're in it, with the jewellery and the new cars, but underneath it all I had very low self-esteem – lower than an ant's.

I met John Fogarty in 1986 when I was thirty. He was very good-looking, very charming. Some guys exude power because of the clothes they wear, the car they drive, but with John it was simply how he conducted himself.

He had a place in Florida, drove a Mercedes and gave waitresses hundred dollar tips. At first I thought he made all his money from his construction company, an excavation firm, but I soon found out he was involved in dealing drugs. First marijuana and then large quantities of coke which he brought to New York through a Florida connection. He'd pick up the coke, wrap it up like a birthday present and bring it on the plane in his carry-on bag. Being Irish, he wasn't actually in the mob, but he was as closely connected as it's possible to be.

John got on well with my little brother Johnny, who'd been a criminal all his life and committed his first murder at eighteen. He'd shot a rival drug dealer in the back of the head and disposed of the body in a patch of wasteland. Afterwards my mother had insisted on being taken to see the body to make sure he'd done it right. I didn't like the idea of the two of them working together. I knew it could come to no good.

But at first business prospered. I was wrapped in fur and bedecked with jewels, jetting around the country like I was the princess of Staten Island. I used to tell my girlfriends that if I couldn't have a manicure, a pedicure and a massage at least three times a week, life wasn't worth living.

The problem was, John not only dealt drugs, he started using them too, going off on long coke binges where I wouldn't know where he was, or who he was with. It got to the point where the real loves in John's life were me, and using and selling cocaine.

I had no illusions about the business my brother Johnny and John were involved with and I knew they'd killed people or had people killed. Once you'd killed with somebody it was like getting married, a kind of private ceremony.

John had a Cuban associate, Aldo, whom I really liked. He always treated me with respect and was fond of my kids (by this stage I had two sons from previous relationships).

Aldo used to come up from his home in Florida every couple of months for 'business' and stay with us. One night in June 1987, Aldo disappeared. What I didn't know was that Aldo had tried to rip John off over a business deal a few months before, and John had ordered him to be killed. John would later claim that he had called off the hit at the last minute, but it had gone ahead anyway. Whatever the case, John came home one day wearing Aldo's watch – a beautiful vintage Patek Philippe. I never asked him about it.

On more than one occasion John came home with blood all over his clothes, which I then had to wash for him. And once he came home for dinner with blood on his shoes, saying he had two bodies in the trunk of his car. A different time he came back to our place on Staten Island and I could tell something unusual had happened. I heard the shower running upstairs and headed up. The bathroom was filled with steam and John's clothes were in a pile on the floor. I knew that he'd killed somebody. I could just tell. I didn't have to ask, and he didn't have to tell me what to do. I took his wallet and keys out of his trouser pocket then I picked up all his clothes, ignoring the smell of gunpowder, and took them into the bedroom. Then I found a plastic garbage bag and stuffed everything into it, including his belt.

As John's addiction to drugs worsened, the distance between us grew. Even the birth of our son Keith in February 1989 didn't bring us closer together. John's moods were wild and unpredictable, and grew more so as business faltered and he stopped making as much money as he had before.

When his erratic behaviour started to endanger the

kids, I took out a restraining order against him. For two weeks he stayed away, but one night he came back, and it was obvious he'd been on one of his binges.

'John, I don't want you here,' I told him.

He stood up and said: 'I'll put a bullet right in your head.' Then he pulled out a nine-millimetre gun from the waistband of his trousers and held it to my head, threatening to kill me, the kids and then himself.

And yet still I took him back. The truth was I loved him like I'd never loved a man before.

On Christmas Eve 1990, our daughter Brittany was born but any hopes that her birth would set John on the straight and narrow were short-lived.

John and Johnny were trying to get back into the big money with a hundred-thousand-dollar pot deal. They needed to raise the money fast, but had only scraped together $30,000. John really wore me down and in the end I signed papers agreeing that if he borrowed the rest of the money from a loan shark and didn't come through with the cash after the transactions, I would have to pay him back myself by selling my house.

What John didn't realise was it was all a set up. The guy had been acting as an informant for the DEA and our phones had been tapped the whole time. On 7 November 1991, John was arrested. After plea-bargaining, he received a sentence of eight years.

Meanwhile, I had to pay back the loan shark. A lot

of people owed John money for drugs, and my brother Johnny went round calling in the debts, and then re-investing the money in deals he and John had set up.

In July 1992, Johnny came round. He told me he had a nagging suspicion he was being followed, that the DEA was watching him.

Immediately after that, I started to notice a lot of strange cars going up and down our block but I didn't think much of it.

On the day the kids were due to go back to school after the summer break, the phone rang at five to six in the morning.

'This is the DEA. Open the door or we're going to break it down.'

I opened the door and by the time I did I could hear agents storming through the kitchen and into the house. There must have been at least fifteen agents in my house, and two of them took me aside and started to read me my rights and the charges against me. 'You are under arrest for conspiracy to distribute cocaine, you are under arrest for . . .'

I was only wearing a thin T-shirt and shorts. I felt degraded, humiliated and very scared – for my kids as much as myself. I kept saying, 'Please let me go to my kids'.

The agents escorted me down the hallway towards Brittany's room and one of them picked her up and was feeling her nappy for drugs. I elbowed him aside and took Brittany away from him, furious that they'd think I'd hide drugs on my baby.

I was taken to Fort Hamilton on Staten Island to be processed, which is where I discovered that twenty-one people had been arrested on Staten Island that morning, amongst them my brother Johnny and his wife Christine.

I didn't understand the drug charges, since nothing was ever in my house. I never had any guns there, and I had never done any dealing myself. As hard as it may be to believe, at that moment I really believed that I hadn't done anything to distribute drugs. I really didn't understand the conspiracy charges.

I kept running the situation through my head. I'd put thirty thousand dollars in the streets. I gave it to John and Johnny to make me back more money. I knew they were investing it in drugs and that I would get my money back, and much more, later on. They took my money to make money selling drugs.

The investigators told me I was facing a long sentence. What freaked me out, though I didn't let on, was that they quoted word for word things I'd said on the phone in talking to John and Johnny. I had never figured that our phones might have been tapped, but it turned out they'd been watching us for months.

Their questions confirmed what I'd suspected. They weren't interested in putting me away as much as they wanted the two Johns and, more importantly, what they knew. They advised me to cooperate with them, tell them what I knew, in return for a lenient sentence.

I didn't want to go to prison, but I knew I could handle myself there. What really worried me was that my kids needed a mother, and what became clear to me was I needed them just as much.

My whole life I'd heard that you never come forward with the truth when dealing with the cops. Lie, lie, lie. That's all I ever heard. And while I wasn't officially in the mob, I knew about the code of silence; it wasn't just a mob thing, it was a street thing. But I wanted to save my ass and take control of my fate. Looking back, that was the first step in saving something more important than my ass – saving my soul.

When John rang from prison, I told him I was going to tell the truth for the sake of my integrity and my honour. I wasn't even going to take a deal, I was just going to tell them everything and I advised him to do the same.

John exploded. 'Are you fucking out of your mind? You can't do that. You'll never get out.'

The DEA needed two witnesses to independently corroborate each other's testimony, in order to put away the other twenty people who'd been arrested that day.

I set about persuading John and Johnny to cooperate with the authorities. Both were hugely reluctant but were eventually persuaded by the threat of jail sentences hanging over both me and Johnny's wife. In return for their full cooperation they were promised their sentences would not be longer than twenty years apiece.

When the formal indictments came down and none of the four of us – the two Johns, Christine or me – were named, everyone knew what had happened.

I was paralysed by fear and uncertainty and my instinct was to cling to what was familiar but the government agents kept telling me I had to get out of my house as they'd picked up on a phone tap that someone was planning on killing me.

I wasn't scared about the hit. I was more afraid of leaving the house that I loved, uprooting my kids from their schools and moving somewhere unfamiliar without a man.

For the kids' sake I didn't want to go into the Witness Protection Program which would have meant living under aliases in a secret location. My son John-John's father had won custody of him, and I was scared of losing him altogether.

But the DEA told me they were relocating me regardless as my life was in imminent danger. We found a place in Bucks County, Pennsylvania, just across the New Jersey state line – a townhouse with three bedrooms.

That was 1992 and, once the charges against me were dropped, we had to start our lives all over again, and I had to find a way of making a living.

Since then, my life has changed drastically. A single

mother, with four children, I somehow managed to keep a roof over our heads, setting up a little cleaning business, then running a B&B and now a small trucking company. I live a quiet, serene life. I practise yoga and go for long walks in the countryside.

The children are grown up and I'm so proud of them. They've done incredibly well. My daughter is a full-time college student. She's highly educated. Sometimes I can't help thinking about how different my life could have been if my parents had educated me. I have lots of regrets on that score, but I refuse to allow them to poison me. I'm going to move forward.

My book came out in 2004 and I have my own website. I do a lot of public speaking, trying to raise awareness of how it is to live in an abusive relationship. I've been amazed how much feedback I've had. I've had women contact me from all over the world, who've been involved with abusive men in some way or another. I tell them to take the time to think about what's happened and to develop strength within themselves.

John and Johnny both entered the Witness Protection Program but John left in 2001 so he could rebuild a relationship with his children. He's built his life up since then, and set up a business. I don't see him on a regular basis, but we keep in touch. I never visited him while he was in prison. I drew a line. I had to for my own sanity.

So much has happened to me over the last few years and, while I wish I'd made different choices earlier in my life, I'm very content with where I am today.

Now when I look back on those years up until 1992, it seems like someone else lived that life. I'm a totally different person now.

Divorced from the Mob *is published by Da Capo Press*

ANNE LEACH

Anne and Carlton Leach live in a cul-de-sac of newly built homes in a village in Essex. Carlton always prefers a cul-de-sac because no one can idly drive past. Despite the difference in ages – Carlton is fifty and Anne twenty years his junior – the two seem settled into a life of easy domesticity with daytime telly playing on the wide-screen TV, washing fluttering in the breeze on the line in the compact garden, and a toy-sized dog making itself very much at home on the sofa. Anne is heavily pregnant when we meet – in marked contrast to the photos of her highly toned lap-dancing days which Carlton proudly shows off – and has since given birth to the couple's first child, Alfie (Carlton has six other children by previous relationships).

Anne wasn't even born when Carlton was first getting into trouble with the law as one of the ringleaders in the organised football violence that flared up in the 1970s and 1980s. From there he followed the well-trodden gangster route running security on the doors of Essex nightclubs and effectively policing the drugs scene in the area with his 'firm' the Essex Boys. When three of his close friends were killed in the infamous Range Rover murders in Rettendon in 1995, Carlton decided to turn his back on the violence, and go straight. Since then, his life has been made into a cult film, Rise of the Footsoldier, *and he has written an autobiography, called* Muscle. *Anne first came face to face with the truth about her new husband's violent past at the Leicester Square premiere of* Rise of the Footsoldier. *But for her, Carlton's criminal activities are a foreign country – to which all links have been resolutely severed. Underneath her thick make-up and baby-fine blonde hair, Anne is a determined character, set on giving her son a 'normal' childhood. The couple are hoping that the bar Carlton has just opened nearby, together with his debt-collecting business, will provide a steady income on which to raise little Alfie – and a new direction for the former gangster.*

I had what I would call a very 'normal' upbringing in Essex. My mum and dad are straight, hard-working people. I was brought up to think that, if you want something, you go out and work for it. I still believe in that despite what people might think. My mum and dad didn't buy me everything I wanted. I had to work for it. I never expected it to be handed to me on a plate.

My dad worked for BT all his life. He started as an engineer and went on to become a manager. And my mum had a lot of part-time jobs. She worked in a shop and as a cook in a pub. The work ethic was always there, and I picked that up from them.

I didn't know about gangsters when I was a child – that certainly wasn't the type of thing my parents would talk about. But as I got older and started going out to clubs, often the people I ended up going out with and mixing with did move in those circles. There was a bit of a myth about certain people, but I was never in awe of any of them.

The way I was brought up is that people are just people. Someone who's been in the papers or on the telly is still just a person. You go and talk to them as you would anybody else. My mum and dad never brought me up to put anyone on a pedestal, especially not a man. I was always taught that I was equal to anyone else.

When I left school, I worked for a while as a secretary in the City. My aim was to save up to put a deposit down on a house, so I started topping up my wages by doing lap dancing on the side. I started off in London then did it locally at the weekends. Then I worked out I could get more money doing the dancing than the City job, so I did that full time.

It's funny people always think lap dancing is somehow exploitative or demeaning, but I absolutely loved it. Best job I ever had. It was like going out clubbing every night, only you'd come home with loads of money!

Soon I had enough to get a mortgage on a house and things were going pretty well. I had plenty of money, a job I loved; I wasn't looking for anything else.

Then one night in March 2006, the manager of the club said there was a group coming in to celebrate a birthday, and he mentioned the name Carlton Leach. Even though I'd later tell Carlton I'd never heard of him, just to make sure he didn't get big-headed, I'd actually met him once or twice years before when I was with an ex-boyfriend who vaguely knew him. But that night it didn't really register. All I was interested in was the fact that a big group meant more dances – and more money.

Carlton's group came in quite late. I was walking by and a friend of his stopped me and called me over. 'I'd like you to have a dance with my friend,' he told me, and he paid for Carlton to have a dance with me. It wasn't love at first sight. For a start, it was his forty-seventh birthday and I was only twenty-seven, so there's a twenty-year age gap. But more to the point, as far as I was concerned I was at work and he was a paying customer. I was just there to get money to pay my mort-gage. I wasn't interested in anything else. But after the dance we got chatting, and I started thinking he was really funny – nice and friendly. He didn't come over as a show-off at all. And he seemed genuinely inter-ested in me, asking me lots of questions.

I still didn't let on that I knew who he was or that

I remembered meeting him. I don't like to give anyone a big head. So I asked him questions like 'what do you do for work' and things like that. He said he did 'this and that', and inside I was thinking: I know exactly what you do.

We spent most of the night chatting and at the end he asked if he could take me out. I said 'OK', and he gave me his number. He always jokes now that he had to pay £60 for me to let him give me his number.

When we went out I finally let on that we'd met before and that I had heard a bit about him. He said he remembered meeting me but I'm not sure if he did. I didn't know what to expect when we went out for that first dinner. I knew to a certain extent what he'd done in the past. But because that kind of thing was never a major fascination to me, I knew only a limited amount. I had a vague impression that he had some kind of 'gangster' reputation, but it was never something I'd have gone out of my way to find out so I hadn't formed any preconceived expectations of him. The way I see it, there's no point in being judgemental about anybody. You can hear stuff about someone, rumours about them, and half the time it's all a load of rubbish anyway. You never know until you talk to someone what they're going to be like. If a friend of mine said, 'I don't like so and so', I'd still give them a chance. Then if I don't like them, I don't like them for myself, not because someone else has told me to think like that.

Even though I hadn't been looking for a relationship, things moved very quickly between us after that first date. We saw each other every day. It's really weird because I'd never been the kind of person to rush into things. I'd have always been the one saying 'you must be sensible and take your time'. But right from the start we spent every day together and within two weeks I'd rented out my own house and moved in with him. If someone had told me beforehand I'd be moving in with someone I'd only just met, I'd have said 'no way', but it just seemed like the most natural thing in the world.

My family were accepting of him right from the start although I admit I sort of drip-fed them information about him and what he'd done. But if I'm happy, they're happy. I think some of my friends were a bit worried because it was so out of character for me to rush into anything. Some people asked: 'Do you not think you should be a bit more cautious?', and there were others who told me about things he was supposed to have done; they weren't necessarily scaremongering, but they were warning me to be careful. But I just thought: He's all right with me.

Inevitably, as I got to know Carlton better, I found out more about him. But the person I wanted to get to understand was the person inside. I was never interested in the other part of him, the darker part. I'm not naive enough to think it doesn't exist, because obviously it does, but that was never really the side I saw so I just didn't want to know about it.

Mind you, we did sort out some boundaries, right from the start, so that there was no confusion. I told him very early on that I wanted to live a 'normal' life, and I wasn't interested in anything to do with violence. I said, 'If you're going to live your life like that, that's fine, you go ahead. But that's not how I want to live my life. So if you decide to live that sort of life, I'm not going to be with you.'

He was honest with me. He said, 'This is who I am', and I said, 'Well, this is my line. If you go over that, we're finished. I don't want things coming in my home that I don't feel comfortable with. I don't want to be worrying where are you, what's happening, who are you with, are you going to come home. I don't want to live my life like that.' I think it helped that, right from the start, there was no confusion about what I would and wouldn't accept.

Mind you, even after establishing those ground rules, there were some things about being with Carlton that I just had to get used to – like the way he checked out places before we went in, standing in the doorway and doing a quick scan with his eyes, and his slight paranoia about going anywhere new – all throwbacks to his old life.

We'd only been together about a month when he proposed. It came completely out of the blue. We'd gone out for lunch and then he said, 'Will you marry me?' I was completely taken aback. In fact, at first I thought he was joking. But when I realised he was serious I said, 'Yes.' Despite only having known each other such a short time. It just felt right. Afterwards, we went to a jeweller's and I chose a ring.

When I told my mum, she was a little surprised but she just said, 'You're old enough to know what's best for you, and if he makes you happy, I'm pleased for you.' My parents know I'm level-headed and wouldn't have jumped into anything without being sure it was right.

I carried on working at the lap-dancing club right up until the wedding, as I really valued my financial independence. In fact Carlton used to come in some nights, and I was impressed at how controlled he was. Not many men could watch their girlfriends dancing provocatively in front of other men, but he took it all in his stride which I took as a really good sign.

Right from the start I knew I didn't want the big fairy-tale wedding. I was never one of those girls who dreamed of wafting down the aisle in a frothy white dress in front of hordes of admiring people. All I wanted was to be with him, and to have a private ceremony that would mean something to us.

Also, I knew that if we had a 'proper' wedding, it would turn into a circus. Carlton knows so many people it would have turned into a huge show wedding. He's been best man nine times, there would have been no way of keeping numbers down. And he would have felt obliged to be on show all day, being larger than life. It would have been like we were getting married for everyone else, not for us. I didn't want that. Besides, I'm the youngest of three so my mum and dad had already been to two weddings.

So, six months after we'd met, we slipped away up to Scotland, just the two of us, and got married in beautiful Comlongon Castle. There's a manor house next door where we stayed in a gorgeous room with a four-poster bed. The actual wedding ceremony was in the castle next door, which was candlelit and atmospheric with a big log fire. I wore a lovely white dress and we said the traditional vows, and it really meant something because it was just the two of us there. We weren't playing to some crowd, or having to live up to anyone else's expectations. It was absolutely perfect.

After the wedding, we went to Ibiza on honeymoon, which was a bit more sociable, but still I tried to keep it as low-key as possible. We went out a few times, but I didn't want to spend my whole honeymoon clubbing so we also had lots of romantic meals and a few evenings just staying in the hotel suite.

I think the wedding made Carlton and everyone else see that I'm very much a low-maintenance kind of girl – I just don't go in for the footballers' wives-type extravaganzas. I don't need all that to feel good about myself.

Of course it's nice to have a few designer clothes but it's what you're like inside that matters. I was never one of those women who want to be bought things all the time. I'd rather Carlton was with me than going out trying to raise the money for me to have all this stuff I don't really need.

I'd never start demanding things from him. That's just not who I am – I'm too much my own person. If he ever went out and did something that got him into trouble I don't want the responsibility of people thinking it was me pressurising him into that to support my lavish lifestyle.

About six months after we got married, filming started on a film about the earlier part of Carlton's life. It was called *Rise of the Footsoldier* and it dredged up a whole load of very difficult memories for him. That was quite a tough time in our relationship. He then reverted back to the person he'd been and that was quite hard. It brought up all those raw emotions.

He wanted to be quite heavily involved with the making of the film, and I can see why, but in some ways it dragged a lot of things up for him that he'd managed to bury. He became very moody. Everything I did would be wrong. All the things that had happened would be playing on his mind and I would have to deal with his bad temper.

I was really thrown in at the deep end because we'd only just been through the lovey-dovey stage and then

I had to deal with that moody person I didn't really recognise. Ultimately, it made our relationship stronger because I knew him better, but at the time it was very hard to deal with.

The worst part was when they were filming the scenes about the Range Rover murders at Rettendon when Carlton's best friend Tony Tucker was killed along with two others. At first I didn't think he should go along to see the filming of the murder scenes but then I started worrying about the effect it would have on him seeing it for the first time in the finished film, so I started thinking that maybe if he watched it being filmed with all the make-up, it wouldn't affect him so much.

It was a really, really difficult thing for him to go through, but it was like a bit of therapy. He revisited some of these very dark memories, and in a way he was then able to put them to bed. But it was very hard.

Tony's death affected Carlton very badly. He took me to visit the grave and I know it's really important to him, but though it might sound quite unfeeling, I don't let him think about it too much because then he gets too deep about it all and it makes him unhappy. I say to him: 'It's happened and nothing can change that. Tony will always be your friend and no one can ever take that away but you can't be living your life thinking about it all the time, or it'll end up ruling you and I don't think that's healthy.'

I didn't know Tony and I can't pretend I did because

Entrance to the Courtneys' sex dungeon

Jenny Courtney in sex dungeon

Jenny and Dave

Judy Marks

Judy and
Howard's
wedding –
from *Mr Nice
and Mrs Marks*
by Judy Marks

Jackie 'Legs' Robinson and Johnny 'Mad Dog' Adair –
from *In Love with a Mad Dog* by June Caldwell and Jackie
'Legs' Robinson

Anne and
Carlton Leach

Anne in her
lapdancing days

Anne in her
lapdancing days

Anne and Carlton at their wedding

Anna Connelly and Viv

Becky Loy

Lyn and Terry
© *Claire Louise Diggins*

Flanagan with nude portrait

Flanagan with signed photo of the Kray Twins

that would make me a hypocrite. People who knew him can talk to Carlton about him but you get a lot of people who've seen the film or they've heard about Tony. They talk to Carlton and I think they try to pull on his heart strings a little bit and I don't like it when they do that. They don't even know him and they're trying to manipulate him for their own reasons. That's not right.

Growing up in Essex, I'd known about the murders for years. Everyone in Essex knew about it all when it happened, so that part of the film wasn't a shock. In fact none of it was a shock really, because I'd prepared myself before I went to see it at the premiere. I knew I'd be seeing things I wasn't going to like. Even so, there's a big difference between knowing something in your head and seeing it visually on the big screen. It was so bloodthirsty. I didn't really like it, to be honest. That sort of violence isn't something I'd normally go to see.

I think it helped that the events in the film ended fifteen years ago. In a way, because he was so much younger then, I can accept it more. I'd only have been fifteen then, so it does seem like a different era. I'm not saying Carlton is an angel now or anything, but he has moved on from that excess of lifestyle in so many ways. You can't carry on living your life with all the violence, the fights. If he'd been behaving in that way now I wouldn't be married to him. Anyway, he's fifty years old now and if he was still acting like that it wouldn't be right. It's OK when you're thirty and you can say you're on a learning curve, but when you're fifty and behaving like that, it's a bit different.

My parents didn't go to see the film at the time, which I was quite relieved about, although my dad has seen it since. I warned him it was quite violent, but he seemed to take it in his stride. My mum still hasn't seen it. She wouldn't like it, and I think it's probably best she doesn't go too deeply into that side of Carlton's life.

I think in some ways I'm also guilty of burying my head in the sand about the violence in his past. There are a lot of things I'd rather be kept in the dark about. I just tell Carlton that I don't want to know about those things. Even today, if there was anything going on I'd probably rather not know about it. Anyway, even though it sounds horrible, if anything like that *was* still happening now, I know it wouldn't actually be Carlton himself doing those things. I say to him: 'I don't want that coming in my house.' Carlton knows there are certain things I don't agree with. He knows I don't want to be living my life through money earned in violent ways. That's not what I want.

When the film came out there was a lot of publicity and since then Carlton does get recognised a lot. We can go to the supermarket, and people will come up to him. It's actually quite sweet normally, they'll say, 'Oh, you're that man from the film'. They're always quite friendly.

In some ways I can't understand it though – that whole 'celebrity' side of his life. The idea that he's got fans is just weird to me. As far as I'm concerned, he's just Carlton. But I know there are people who are interested in that way of life and who buy those kinds of books and see those films and obviously think he's someone.

To be honest, I think it's bizarre that people become celebrities from doing violent things. But with Carlton, he's also got the likeability factor. He's friendly. He's not a miserable sod. He's funny. But sometimes I do look at him when he's doing one of his shows or book signings and think: But what have you actually done?

I suppose people are into that whole gangster thing at the moment. It's cool. People are always curious about the 'other side' of life and it's intriguing to them. I guess everyone has different interests. For some people, reading about all this stuff is almost like a hobby. I like horse riding, they like gangsters. At the end of the day they're the people who buy the tickets. But it is glamorising it. People see films and documentaries, all this stuff about money and everything, and they're really fascinated by it. They're won over by the lifestyle they imagine these people are leading.

Carlton loves the attention. He goes round doing these shows where they talk about the film and sign books and have photos taken with people in the audience. But then he comes home and it's just normal. I wouldn't have him coming home all big-headed and swanning around. I'd say, 'Did you have a nice time? Now how about getting into the kitchen and starting dinner?' Everyone likes to be adored. But it brings out the show-off in him – then I think it's my job to make him grounded. Sometimes it makes me laugh because the people who see the shows or the films must think we lead this fabulous life with non-stop champagne and parties. People see the films and they think we must be loaded. They don't think about the mortgage and the bills we've got to pay.

I've got my head screwed on financially. That comes from my upbringing. My parents were very much of the opinion: 'if you can't afford it, you've got to save up for it'. In that way I think I've been quite good for Carlton. Since we've been together I've been keeping his spending under control. I've been saying, 'Come on, you can't buy this or that. How much have we got . . .'

When we met he didn't have a mortgage or anything like that. It was day-to-day living. I thought: Well, if that's how you want to live your life, that's fine, but you're not getting any younger, you need to be putting towards something. So now he's a little bit more sensible. He always makes sure everything is paid, before splashing out on anything. If I was the kind of person who was always wanting things and asking for things, he'd never say, 'No, you can't have that', but then he'd be like, 'Well, now I've got to go and do X to pay for that'. Whereas I'd rather wait until we can afford it.

Carlton has six kids from previous relationships to support financially as well. He was quite open about his kids right from the first date, although I admit it was a bit of a shock when he first told me. 'You've got *how* many kids?' I asked him, completely stunned. The way I deal with it is to group them into those who are grown-up and those who are still 'children' – that way it's easier to cope with. Obviously they're all still his children, but the younger children are the ones I have the main contact with – they come to the house and they stay or whatever. The older ones are more independent – if they want to come and see him, they come and see him. His eldest son is older than me but with the younger children you've got to be patient and build up a relationship. Like all kids they'll try it on sometimes, but I think they know the boundaries now and it's all fine.

Carlton was only married once before, but he had other serious relationships. I try to be the grown-up one about the exes. To be honest, if you're going to be difficult, the only one you make things hard for in the end is yourself. I just think: I want the easy life. I'll go along, smile, be friendly.

Workwise, Carlton is doing a few different things at

the moment. As well as the shows, he has just opened a bar and he also runs a legitimate debt-collection business working with a friend who's a bailiff. In some ways it would be nice if he had a nine to five job and everything would be more secure and I'd know where he is and where he's going, but he would never be happy living like that. He could do it, but I'd find myself sharing a house with Victor Meldrew.

I'd like to think the bar will eventually start running itself. The honest truth is I'd prefer him to cut down the hours there, but he's still building it up. When it's financially viable they'll get other people in to run it for them.

Anyway, I'm not so naive that I think he's going to change the habits of a lifetime. He was old enough when I met him that I'd have been stupid to think I could go in and change him. He was forty-seven years old. That's who he was. That was him. Take it or leave it.

I think people would be quite surprised at how boring our life is. I think people assume we're out every night, champagne, dinner. But our life is just normal. We have to do the food shopping every week. Most nights we stay home and watch the telly. He goes to work and does his thing, I stay here and do the cleaning, he comes home and cooks the dinner.

If I meet new people, I never say anything about what Carlton does or what he's done in the past – I just say he has a debt-collection company and leave it at that. I just want us to be 'normal'.

Of course I still like going to the swish clubs, but I've done all my going out when I was younger. When I used to work in the clubs I went out a lot. Nowadays I'll go every now and then, but I can take it or leave it. At the end of the day, that life's not real. It's nice to go out and have a nice time and have nice drinks, but week in and week out that's not a real life, I don't think. It's very false.

When you're going out doing that stuff, you attract a certain type of 'friend' and I use the word loosely. It's all the people who are the hangers-on. Carlton does sometimes tend to attract people who I don't think are necessarily good for him. I think all women are a bit better at judging people. Out of the two of us, Carlton is the one who's straight up front, whereas I've always held back. I'm the one who sits and waits, thinking I'll take my time to work out what this person's like, whereas his nature is he'll jump in straight away and they'll be best friends immediately. And I'll sometimes say to him, 'Just be a little bit cautious. Give him a wide berth for a little while', and it tends to die off a bit. Carlton will know if I don't like someone. I'll smile and be polite and then I'll tell him not to get too involved. But at the end of the day, that's his choice. I can only advise. Sometimes I've learned the best thing to do with him is to let him do it. The more I say no the more he'll go and do it, whereas if I just say once, 'Well, I don't think it's a good idea', he'll think it through in his head and eventually come to the conclusion I might be right.

I'm not bothered about going to clubs. I'd rather stay in and have dinner and drinks, just the pair of us. Or maybe go out and have something to eat with friends. There are some times when I'll be invited along for a night out and I won't want to go because I know it's going to be one of those evenings with lots of men with egos and too much testosterone. If the other girlfriends and wives are there, and they're my friends, I'll go, but I don't want to go to certain things. I just want a normal life.

I know there are always people who are attracted to Carlton because of who he is or who they think he is. Young girls think going out with a 'gangster' is a fantastic life. They think it's all about drinking champagne and being bought jewellery every day, but the reality would come as such a shock. Sure you can be bought nice things and everything, but there's a lot more to it than that. But they don't know that so if he goes to a club on his own, there's always some girl who'll try it on. It used to bother me, but now the way I deal with it is to think: We're married. If he's stupid enough to fall for that, it wouldn't be my loss, it'd be his loss. He's always quite friendly, Carlton, but he knows where the line is and I think he'd keep away. When you're married,

I think you have to trust each other, otherwise what kind of a life do you have? I go out on my own, he goes out on his own. We have to have faith in each other.

I do worry in some ways about him getting bored with being settled and normal. You can't change someone's personality; I can't tell him to be a certain way. But Carlton knows the situation with me. He knows that if it got to the stage where I was unhappy and he was out all the time, every night, I'd say, 'Well, what's the point of being married to you?' I think hopefully he's old enough to realise. On the other hand, when do men grow up?

I know people have this image of the glamorous gangster's wife and, to be honest, there is a certain amount of pressure to look good, but that pressure comes as much from me as from him. At the moment I'm about to have a baby and I've gained weight and I wouldn't go out to a club until I'm looking more like myself. Not that Carlton would ever say 'you're not coming out like that, until you've lost weight' but I know that deep down he wants me to look nice. It's part of what attracted him to me. He doesn't want me to go out in my sweatpants with my hair scraped back. Even though he's not shallow and I'm sure he'd love me whatever, I'm a realist and I know the looks thing is part of the whole package. But there's only so long you can look at the cover before you have to have a look inside.

It's all well and good being a so-called 'trophy wife', but you've got to have a bit of a brain as well. Carlton knows that we can go out and I would never embarrass him. He knows he could leave me with people to have a conversation and it would be a sensible conversation. I wouldn't be saying stupid things and showing off and saying he does this or that. I'm intelligent and grown-up enough. Part of being presentable is being a bit clued up and knowledgeable and using your brain. You can have someone who's all dollied up and doesn't know what they're saying and they'll end up dropping you in it. I'd never do that.

The thing is I've never put Carlton on a pedestal. We're equals. I don't see him as anything other than him. To me he's not a caricature. I see him as Carlton, the person I live with, the person I go food shopping with. I would never be in awe of him. I think men might want the dolly bit for a little while but then they'd get bored and want someone who could have a conversation. Carlton knows he can't get away with things around me. I keep him grounded.

That's why the people close to Carlton are happy for him since he's been with me. His best friends like Sid and Kevin have been in his life for twenty or thirty years and they're the only ones whose opinion I'm bothered about. They're all happy for him because he's happy.

I think there are probably some people who don't

like the fact that he's not out all the time any more, but he can't be doing that for the rest of his life. He's fifty years old. When does it stop? He's got to be allowed to be happy and settled too.

Carlton and I try to go to our place in Spain whenever we can. We have a place in Almeria – right away from the Costa del Sol. His kids go there and his mum and dad. It's in a little town. When we go there we can just relax. That's where he is just Carlton. We can go out to the beach and he doesn't have to act a certain way or be a certain way. He can just be him. If it was Marbella or somewhere like that it would be a different story because he'd still have to play that part of being Carlton Leach. But when we go to Almeria you can literally see him relax. He doesn't have to be anybody but himself.

I don't know how our lives are going to change once the baby is born. I know there might be some awkward questions up ahead when he or she is a bit older, about the things Carlton used to do.

To be honest, I just want a normal, stable upbringing for my child. People can be judgemental about things they don't know anything about. I don't want anyone saying to my child 'your daddy used to do this or that'. Carlton is straight now. He's got his legitimate businesses.

The film is out there, it's in the public domain, so I'd have to bring the kids up to be a little clued up and gradually drop in things about what Carlton has done, as and when they're old enough to understand. The way I'd envisage it, I'd start off with them knowing 'Daddy works in a bar', which already makes it different from 'Daddy works in an office', and then I'd gradually add to the picture. Then when they get to be a teenager I could say, 'Daddy used to do this, a long time ago'.

But I wouldn't want any child of mine looking back on the way Carlton used to be and thinking it was cool. If I had a son, I wouldn't want to encourage him to think that was a good way to behave or to have people around who'd encourage him to think that. I don't think Carlton would want that for his son either. His eldest son is a born-again Christian and Carlton's quite happy that he's gone that way because at least he knows where he is at night, and he knows he's safe. He wouldn't want that other life for his child.

People who've seen the film sometimes do ask me if I ever worry that there might be a side to Carlton I haven't seen yet and the answer is 'yes'. Do you ever know someone 100 per cent? Isn't there always a bit that you don't know? Obviously I know he can be moody and he can have a temper, but there may be another part of him hidden away, and to be honest, that's the bit I wouldn't want to know.

He has got a temper. He's got a very bad temper. It's ugly. Sometimes Carlton's temper seems to come out of nowhere. If we're driving along and someone cuts in front of us, it's awful. Carlton's someone with a long memory. He'll say, 'Right, if I see that car again . . .' and he would actually remember. I'm always the one trying to calm things down, but there have been instances before where there have been altercations. I hate that. I'd rather he shouted at me than get into something with someone else.

Some days he's got more tolerance than others. If something's bothered him previously or something's playing on his mind that's happened, and someone cut in front of him on the road and got him on a bad day, that's when the ugly side will come out. Whereas if he's happy, then there's more chance that it'll just go over his head.

I don't like that side of him, the angry side. I tend to try to ignore it. If he's like that with me, I think the best thing is to try to ignore him. Then the only person he's arguing with is himself. I tell him to go out. If he's really angry, he leaves the house and he'll drive round the block or something and that's the way he'll deal with it. I've got quite a temper as well. I say to him, 'Either you go out or I'll go out and we'll calm down and then we'll talk about it.' Better that than have a big heated argument. Or I'll tell him to go into the other room, so that the situation becomes defused. That's the way I deal with it.

I've never been scared of him though. If I was ever

scared of him I wouldn't be with him any more. He does actually understand that if he ever lost it completely with me, then I wouldn't be his wife any more. That's why he'd rather just go out. More than half the time I'll point out he's not actually angry with me, he's angry with someone else and taking it out on me.

There are always people who want to make a name for themselves by trying to start something with Carlton. It's some kind of kudos. They think they can go off and say, 'I got into a fight with that so-called hard man'. They're trying to get themselves a reputation. They're idiots. I have seen him lose his temper really badly before when we've been out. That upsets me far more than anything else. I can't explain it; he goes from one thing to something completely different – it's so extreme. It's upsetting and horrible. I think he doesn't want me to see that. He doesn't want me to see him lose control.

People won't do something directly to him, they'll do it to someone he's with to get his back up. It's really underhand. Like one time when we were out, some bloke came up and started making racist comments to a friend of Carlton's we were with who was Indian. Well, Carlton just completely lost it.

I was telling him to let it go but when he's in that state, he's like an animal, you can't grab him back. He goes crazy – not so much at the other person but just on his own – punching his hands through glass, head-butting something, blood everywhere. It's horrible really. It's frightening. I think: if he can do that to himself, what else is he capable of? But in a weird way, he's trying to calm himself down by doing it, trying to stop himself hitting out at anybody else.

After that time with that bloke I said to him, 'If you're going to carry on like that, we haven't got a future.' People were ringing up the next day and thinking what happened was cool and it wasn't at all. There's all this ego stroking, 'oh, you were this and you were that', and they're all talking about it amongst themselves, but I don't think that's any way to behave. It upsets me. I've said to him: 'Don't do that again.'

Since then I've developed an antenna so I can tell if something is going to happen, or someone is going to cause trouble, and I'll say, 'Let's go home'. I won't give a reason, I'll just say I want to move on. If he's with someone I trust as a friend, I'll say, 'Why don't we say this to him, to try to get him away and defuse the situation because it's going to build up otherwise.' I have to do it in a way so he's not aware that's what I'm doing. I have to do it subtly. Otherwise he'd think I was making him look like an idiot, telling him what to do. He doesn't like the idea that anyone might think he was under the thumb. In some ways he likes to have a little bit of a rebellion. I can't tell him what to do. He's old enough. But there's a way to persuade him –

usually by making him think something is his own idea!

I try not to get into any situations where anyone might try to chat me up. I remember we went to football once and this young bloke sitting next to me started chatting away, and Carlton came late so he didn't know we were together. But he was really harmless and Carlton could see that so he didn't say anything. Afterwards he said he was quite flattered because this guy was so young. It would be different if someone was grabbing me. But if someone makes a beeline for me now, I just walk away. It might seem rude but I think: I'm actually helping you here, mate.

As time's gone on, I can read him better and I know how to deal with things better. Sometimes I know just to leave something and come back to it in a couple of days. I know how to play it more. Most of the time though, he's happy. He's a good husband. He cooks every day. I'm very lucky. He'll always help with things. Moneywise he looks after everything. If I was ill, he'd look after me. He's caring. He'd make sure I was OK. I know he'll be there when the baby's born and he'll help me. That's his kind, caring side. In some ways he's over-kind to people and then they end up taking advantage of him.

Really we just want to have a quiet life. That's why Carlton is selective about where we go if we go out. He still gets nervous about security. That'll always be part of him. When you've been in the situations Carlton has been in I don't think you ever stop looking over your shoulder, or casing a place before you go in.

But I'd hope that anxiety might ease a bit in time. Things do change don't they, as you get older? Of course Carlton doesn't want to get older. He wants to be Peter Pan. He still keeps himself healthy and fit, although he doesn't go to the gym so obsessively any more. I try to tell him to start focusing on different things, now, like his family. I say, 'Look how lucky you are.'

It's funny, doing things like this book, because I don't see our life as something extraordinary, or Carlton as this big-shot villain. I'm not interested in the myth of him. I'm only interested in the person. The person inside. Not this exaggerated person who's on the telly. As far as I'm concerned Carlton is the man who comes to the supermarket with me or cooks me a Sunday roast. He's not the man on the film. That's not real. This is real – us at home with the dog and the telly and soon with our baby.

You can keep the myth. I'll take the reality any day.

'DONNA'

Donna is forty-seven, with carefully highlighted blonde hair, and a downright dirty laugh. Originally from California, she now lives quietly in Brighton with her fourteen-year-old daughter Mae. During the 1990s, Mae's father, Mark, was one of the big players supplying Ecstasy on the London rave scene. The fact he'd already served a two-year prison sentence for shooting someone had helped garner him a fearsome reputation in underworld circles. Despite her sheltered upbringing, Donna not only accepted her husband's activities, but enthusiastically participated in them, regularly couriering large quantities of drugs up and down to Scotland. Since her marriage broke down three years ago amid bitter recriminations from both sides, Donna has been struggling for money for the first time in her life and is even considering getting a 'proper' job. She originally agreed to be identified for this book, wanting to act as a cautionary example to any 'naive idiots' like her younger self, but changed her mind at her daughter's insistence. 'I have to accept her wishes. She's been through enough,' she said.

I was a typical Californian all-American girl – blonde, sporty, with a permanent smile on my face. So quite how I ended up living in the East End of London, married to a big-time drug dealer and running thousands of pounds worth of drugs up and down to Scotland is anyone's guess.

I didn't come from a rich background, but I would say I came from a decent background. I did well at school, went to college and came out with a Bachelor of Science degree.

When my mother passed away and left me a decent sum of money, I decided to go travelling for a few months. I had an enquiring mind and wanted to see more of life than just the place I'd grown up in.

I met Mark in London. I was in a club called City of Angels, which I thought was quite ironic seeing as I come from Los Angeles. I thought he was the most striking man I'd ever seen in my life. Even after everything we've been through I have to admit he's a handsome bastard. He's very unusual-looking, mixed-race and at that time had a head of dreadlocks. To me at twenty-three, he was really exotic. Of course I had no idea he'd just come out of a two-year stretch in prison for shooting someone.

I just walked straight up to him and said, 'Hi. You

look like you're having some fun.' Pretty cool line, huh? Not. He turned round to me and asked, 'Do you want something to drink?' I replied, 'Yes, please', and then promptly ran to the bar and bought it myself. He must have thought he had it made!

We didn't chat that much. He wasn't really a conversationalist. He asked me if I wanted a smoke. I'm not really a puffer, but I said yes because I wanted to be with him. We went outside and sat down on a staircase and he rolled a spliff, then turned around and offered it to me (which I learned later was very unusual for him – he'd roll a second joint for other people but he *never* shared). He was really taken aback when I said, 'Oh no, I don't smoke.' I don't think he could make me out at all.

To me, he was exciting. He was so different from anyone else I'd met, but I didn't think he was really interested in me, I thought he was just being friendly because of my accent. I was really naive.

I ended up staying at his house because I was too drunk to get back to where I was staying. He tried it on but when I said 'no' he backed straight off. I was surprised he even tried as I really didn't think he fancied me.

As it turned out, he was babysitting for a friend who was having a termination. Her man had been in prison and was coming out for a little break so she needed to get rid of the baby double-quick. So he was looking after this other child, whom I didn't meet until the next morning.

What I didn't realise then was that the house I was staying in was a halfway house for prisoners who'd just been released. I spent most of the day with Mark and the child. I was hung-over and seeing double, and we were just hanging out. Then he just turned round and said something very casually and randomly like, 'Well, you know I just got out of the nick after two years.' I thought: whoa – but by the time I'd collected my thoughts, he'd walked out of the room. I was sitting there thinking: Oh well, he's probably just shoplifted something. But when I pressed him, I found out he'd shot somebody. He'd been in the papers and everything.

It turned out this pimp thought Mark was messing around with one of his girls. I think the main attraction to this girl was that she had a mixed-race son that Mark had become quite close to. But this guy thought that Mark was moving in on his territory. The guy basically pistol-whipped him and broke his jaw. Mark shot him in the leg, but then immediately put a tourniquet on him and called the ambulance.

The newspapers actually gave him a fairly good press because he'd acted in self-defence and had tried to help, but he ended up doing two years for it.

I didn't know what to think. At the time I thought he was one of the sweetest people I'd ever met. Of course I now wouldn't say that, but back then I'd never met anyone like him. Anyone who'd served a prison term in the United States had always seemed really rough, but he seemed gentle and kind.

I went off travelling to Italy for a bit after that, before returning to London en route back to the States. I called Mark up and ended up staying with him in the halfway house. I had all these men around me, and just a communal bathroom, but they were so nice and respectful. They'd say, 'Oh, Donna, do you want some tea?'

I remember telling my girlfriend where I was and she said, 'Have you lost all sense of reality? Have you gone mad?', and I said, 'No, no, they're the nicest people you'd ever want to meet.'

By that stage something had happened between Mark and me, but I was still determined to go home. As far as I was concerned it was a holiday fling.

I returned to the States and set up a business organising visas and passports for people who were travelling. It was pretty time-consuming, but Mark was still in the back of my mind, and I kept talking to him on the phone. When I got my phone bill I was aghast to find it was $500. I said, 'You know what? I might as well send you a ticket to come over here, the amount of money I'm spending on calls.'

So he came over to the States. He didn't really know what he was going to do or how long he was going to stay, and it was quite a difficult time because he couldn't work legitimately, so I was the complete breadwinner. It was OK, but a little bit of a strain.

Between what my mother had left me and the business, I was doing all right financially, but in any relationship where one partner relies on the other in a way that isn't balanced, there's going to be friction. After about three months of this, I'd had enough. 'Maybe we should get married,' I suggested, wearily. That way, he could get his green card and legitimately work and everything would be better. Or so I thought. I wasn't madly in love with him. It was a convenience thing. It was to buy us more time so that we could see how we got along living a 'normal' life.

So we did the Las Vegas thing. The wedding day was wild. I had an antique Victorian silk black dress – black, that should have told me something, don't you think? We were married by this Seventh-Day Baptist woman preacher who overcharged us. We argued about money for about half an hour before and after the service.

We actually were supposed to get married on Friday, 13 June, just before midnight, but because we argued so much, we finally said our vows in the first minutes of Saturday the fourteenth. You'd have thought that might have been a good omen but it didn't turn out that way. I can't even remember the year any more, probably around 1989.

Anyway, afterwards we walked out, changed into more appropriate clothing, then we sat in Caesar's and started gambling. We could really only afford for one of us to gamble, and Mark is really a bit of a card shark. We sat down at the blackjack table and got hit on by this gorgeous couple, who obviously were into swinging. I thought that was kind of a weird start to a marriage, being propositioned about wife swapping. In the end we told them thanks but no thanks and played cards and drank until we were ready to pass out. The next day, Mark insisted we had consummated the marriage, but all I remember is the passing out.

It was basically more of an arrangement than a marriage. But Mark did say to me, 'If we do decide to get married for real, we'll do it in a church back in England.' Later I called him on that, and he said, 'Why would we do that? We've been together ten years now', and the moment was gone.

We'd decided we would move to Chicago after the wedding, but those plans changed when Mark flew back to England for a holiday and couldn't get back into the States after the immigration authorities checked into his records. So then we were apart for a few months, which wasn't exactly ideal for newly-weds! But we were talking on the phone a lot, and finally I decided to go over to England for a holiday.

By the time I went, we'd been apart for six months, and in that time he'd got right back into the swing of things for the first time after coming out of prison and he had become The Man. It was the heyday of the rave scene. There were people making money hand over fist out of Ecstasy. He wasn't the guy on the corner selling them. He wasn't the guy in the pub selling them. He was the guy supplying the whole show. The head honcho.

Everywhere we went, people knew who he was. We'd go to clubs and the doormen knew him because they bought in their own supplies from him, so wherever we went we were shown straight in. We never had to queue anywhere. And because he had this reputation after shooting someone, everyone was scared to death of him. In those days nobody even had a gun, let alone had shot someone with it.

It was a whole new world for me. You'd think I'd be horrified by the idea of being married to a big-time drug supplier, but I was quite thrilled by it all. I was just this little American girl, you know, I'd never known anyone who'd had more than a traffic ticket. It was exciting.

And it wasn't long before that kind of world started to rub off on me. At that time, Mark had people working for him and this woman befriended me who was part of his organisation. We went to some pub and I parked my car right outside. We were having a nice time, minding our own business when all of a sudden this drunk guy jumped up on my car and walked straight over it. It was only a Ford Fiesta, no big deal, but it was the audacity of it that incensed me.

I shouted out, 'Excuse me. That's my car.' The guy just looked at me and continued walking and gave an extra stomp on the boot.

I thought: Oh, *really*? And without even pausing, I got the bottle of beer I was drinking and smashed it over the side of this guy's head. I'd never done anything violent in my life. I could have killed him but it didn't even occur to me.

Luckily this guy survived, and launched himself at me. Then this other guy came over to hold us apart. And the girls I'd been talking to were just looking at each other saying, 'What the hell is she doing?' They dragged me down the street, got me into a cab and got me away.

After that I kept getting messages from people saying, 'Donna, don't go back to that pub. That guy is crazy. He says that if he finds that American bitch, he's going to kill her.' I didn't need telling twice.

Then rumours got back to my husband. I don't know what he did or said, but the next thing I knew, the messages coming back to me from this guy were very different. 'Tell her I'm very, very sorry.' 'Tell her it won't happen again.'

That was the first time I thought: Oh, so that's who I'm married to. That was the first time I realised how known he was, and how scared people were of him. That was the first time I realised who he was, and who I was – and I liked it.

But I was never really involved in the details of what he did. I didn't want to be. I always said to him 'the less I know, the better', so if the heat came down, I wouldn't be tempted to say anything.

I know that on a few occasions, something would go wrong and he and his friend Joe would have to go round to 'sort things out'. What exactly he did to these people who needed 'sorting out' I have never found out to this day, and don't want to find out.

I may not have wanted to delve too deep into how he made his money, but I certainly enjoyed spending it. We had a good lifestyle – moving from home to home as he made more and more money, driving nice cars, eating out all the time. We didn't want for anything. I was never into the designer clothes, so I wasn't exactly swanning around in Prada, but then I was 5 ft 10, under thirty, blonde hair and a body to die for. Who needs Prada? I was a bit of a trophy wife, I guess. I looked a certain way, I was from California, and I was tough too.

Having a social life when you're involved with a gangster is never simple. One week you're friends with guys he 'works' with and you're hanging out with the missus round at their house, and the next week he wants to kill them and they're not allowed in the house. There's no such thing as a real friendship base, which always used to trip my head out because I'm a really hospitable person.

Mark never had any real friends, apart from Joe maybe. They were both really into comics. Mark used to go out and buy £500 comics as gifts for Joe, but they ended up falling out.

To be honest, none of his gangster cronies seemed to really like women much either. Women were just there to be in magazines to jerk off to. I might have looked like a trophy wife but I used to say I could be a cardboard cut-out for all the interest his friends showed in me as a person.

I did sometimes get jealous of other women, because Mark was a very handsome man. But to be honest, the idea of him running off with another woman never really came into my head. He would flirt, of course, he loved to flirt. But then I loved to flirt too, although I'd never do it in his presence. He'd send me out for the night with ten Es and a hundred pounds, and my girl-friends and I would go off and have fun and flirt to our hearts' content.

I found my own group of girlfriends – not the ones he was throwing at me because he wanted to do business with their men. I found good friends that are still my friends today. My friends are PRs, they run their own businesses, they're financial advisors. I'm the only flake in the whole group.

To be honest, I liked the thrill of Mark's world – to the extent that I willingly allowed myself to get involved in it. Now when I look back, I think that he couldn't have loved me to let me do what I did. I could have been thrown into prison. I was trafficking Ecstasy pills up to Aberdeen. I'd have this huge bottle with about 3000 pills just in a carrier bag thing, and I'd take them up. I got paid something paltry like £300. Big deal, right? But I did it for the buzz.

I'd be met at Aberdeen by this couple. I'd give them the stuff, they'd give me dinner, they'd drive me back to the airport and I'd fly home again. I did it so many times the guy who worked at Aberdeen airport started recognising me. 'Oh, you again.' I'd say, 'Oh yes, just going up to see my boyfriend again.' I told myself I was doing it to help Mark, but really it was because it was such a buzz.

The arrangement was that they sent the money on afterwards, so that I didn't travel around with all that cash. But after one trip, they suddenly went silent. No money. Mark was furious but just wanted to track them down. The woman had mentioned she worked in a top hair salon. How many of those could there be in Aberdeen? So while Mark was passed out after a bender the night before, I jumped on a flight to Aberdeen.

At Aberdeen airport I found a cab driver and told him a story about these two whose club we were sponsoring and who owed us money and I needed to find. He was intrigued. He thought it was like a movie. He took me to one salon – I walked in, she wasn't there. Two, not there. Three – as soon as I walked in I saw her. She stopped, and then indicated to me to go downstairs while she finished a client. When she followed me downstairs, she gave me a whole spiel about the money. I said I needed to see her partner. She said, 'No problem. I'll call him now.' As she turned her back on me, it suddenly occurred to me that she could tell him anything – to run, to rescue her, anything. The adrenalin was pumping and as she turned round, I said, 'Listen, if you're thinking of tell him to get out, don't, darling. Because I'm telling you, I'm just the welcoming committee. He won't like what's behind me.'

Even as the words were coming out of my mouth, I couldn't understand where they came from. I've never spoken like that before in my life. Tarantino eat your heart out!

After that they were shitting themselves. They thought I'd been sent up by this gang to deliver the warning and that the whole organisation was hot on my heels. It was hysterical.

The guy drove me in his lorry to the safe house where all his boys were and handed me this wad of money. Any sane person would have grabbed it and run, but I was enjoying my new role too much. I sat there and counted it slowly in front of them, note by note. Then I said, 'Right, I get paid £300 every time I come up here, and I want that and also the flight and the cab money. Oh, and my flight leaves in a couple of hours and I'll need you to take me to the airport.'

I don't know who this enforcer woman was, but she was on fire! He couldn't do enough for me – took me on a mini sightseeing tour, took me to get fish and chips, took me to the airport. Then I went home. There was Mark, still out for the count – and me with this fat bundle of cash in my hand.

I'm a mad woman. I know it. Why was I trafficking shit? I didn't need the money. It was just part of the thrill. In some ways I had the makings of a good criminal, but I couldn't have done some of the things Mark did. Without going into details, I just couldn't have done those things. I was certainly no angel, but I couldn't have done that.

Mark and I had never had an easy relationship, but things started to go badly wrong when he got into doing hard drugs himself instead of just selling them. His behaviour became erratic and unpredictable, and we argued a lot. Then I became convinced he was cheating on me and we split up for a few months.

But I gave Mark a lot of leeway because of the problems he'd had in his life. He was mixed-race but had been adopted by an all-white family. I don't think living in an all-white area in Leeds did him a lot of favours. There's a story about him and his white sister coming home from school in matching uniforms, and the police stopping him and insisting he go 'home' to the black area. She was saying, 'But that's my brother.' Some of his stories pulled on my heart strings. I was constantly using his background to make excuses for him.

When we got back together in 1993 I thought that blip was behind us, and started thinking about having a baby. We'd been together seven years by that stage, and a lot of people were telling me that if I had his baby he'd calm down. I said, 'That's not a good enough reason to bring a child onto this planet.' But after everything we'd been through, I really thought we were over the worst.

For a while after our daughter Mae was born, it seemed I was right. We'd go out into the countryside and take walks, just the three of us. But as she got older that side of things grew less and less. It was like I was stuck on the back burner.

Mark would take off and I wouldn't know where he'd gone. When he came home I wasn't allowed to ask him any questions. He started having a huge problem with crack. Ironically that meant he was home more because, unlike the Es he'd been on before, he couldn't take crack in public.

Our relationship deteriorated in inverse proportion to his burgeoning drug habit. Then my father died and left me another sum of money. We'd always talked about buying a bar somewhere exotic – that was our big dream. So we went to Belize and we nearly bought some property but, even though we were so far from home, Mark still managed to find the local coke dealer. No wonder that deal came to nothing.

Then we remortgaged our flat and we got the place next door and fixed it up. I thought that would give him a focus, get him away from the drugs. But I was wrong.

His drug use escalated and, as it did, his business suffered.

A lot of guys he used to deal with cut him off because of the drugs. Suddenly we weren't making the money we used to. Some of the guys he'd worked with would still hang out with us socially – our families would still get together. But as far as business went, they cut him out. They weren't sending any work his way.

Mark became increasingly moody and violent towards me. Now that I've got a lovely boyfriend who treats me well, I question myself all the time now about why I put up with it. But you have to look at it in context. There was a lot of drugs in my home. There was a lot of madness around. We went through so much money with nothing to show for it.

It wasn't even as if our sex life was that good. It was never that kind of passionate relationship, we never had make-up sex after our arguments. So why didn't I just cut my losses and leave?

One reason was fear, I guess. Fear of being on my own, fear of what Mark would do. He frightened me.

Two was lifestyle – even though we weren't making the big money any more, we still made a living, and I'd never really had a job. And three, we had a daughter together. I guess I thought I had to keep us together for her. He was a good dad when he was up.

I tried to convince myself I was right to stay with him and put up with it. I'd never been in love before in my life. I was naive. I told myself that he needed me. To this day I don't know whether I was ever in love with him. I don't even know if I believe in love. Do you know where the phrase 'head over heels' comes from? If you were caught being a philanderer in the olden days, you'd be tied with your arms behind your back, and your legs brought up sharp behind you until your back snapped in half. Literally 'head over heels'. I like that explanation because I believe there's an element of violence involved when you love someone passionately. I was certainly afraid of him. And I was probably addicted to him in a way. Who knows? Now I'm forty-seven and I'm thinking: Shit. I gave that man half of my life and he treated me like that.

The arguments grew worse and worse and he ended up dumping me twice in one year. What silly bitch gets dumped twice in a year?

We were living in Leytonstone in this huge house I'd redesigned, and we had an argument and he said, 'That's it. I'm gone', and he packed his bags and left. He'd left behind £5000 in cash and I thought 'whoopee let's party'. I invited friends round and we had a ball.

My friends were great – they never dictated what I should do but they were there for me when they needed to be. They're smart enough to know that they couldn't have told me to get out of that relationship before I was ready. They all knew I was bright enough to work it out for myself.

Looking back, Mark probably had another woman even then, but I didn't know about it and, like a fool, when he came knocking, I took him back. But I was determined things were going to be different. I'd already invested some of the money I inherited from my dad in a property on the south coast and I decided I wanted to move there permanently. Make a clean break. I've always lived my life like it was some kind of novel – playing up the excitement, not thinking it was too real. But then you have a kid and you realise you have to get some security into your life. The plan was I would move with Mae and then Mark would join us eventually. I certainly didn't see it as leaving him. He even helped with the moving in August 2006.

It was Christmas Day of that year when I realised things weren't quite going to work out that way. I'd had a few drinks, and was sitting there with my little girl when he rang up. I thought he was phoning to tell me when he was arriving but instead he told me he'd met someone else and was leaving me.

I went crazy. I lost it. I'm not proud of myself with

my daughter sitting right there. But, hell, Christmas Day is not a great time to tell your wife you're leaving her. He had gone to rehab by that time and all I could think about was how he'd finally got himself straightened up – just in time to leave me for someone else.

It took me a while to get over that. I still have trouble. I look at my daughter, who's fourteen, and I think, You know what? No matter what, it was worth it, just for her. But I can't help looking back and thinking what an idiot I was.

I look at my life and ask where it came from – this crazy psychotic streak. I had a normal upbringing, finished school, got my education. What made me take the course I did?

I love to write, and in a way my whole life has been like a novel. I make things happen so that I can go home and write about them afterwards. My first boyfriend said that to me: 'You know what, you can't wait for things to be over so you can look back on them.' And it's true. I've wanted my life to be stranger than fiction. I'm an excitement junkie, an adrenalin junkie. I can't help it. But now I'm trying to rein that in.

These days I just want an easy life. I'm tired of drama. I've got a new boyfriend, Simon, who has helped me see what a nice man can be like and I think to myself: Why on earth did I give that guy seventeen years? That's what gets me bitter. But you know, I have my little girl.

And apart from my finances, which are dire, I'm actually happier than I've been in my entire life.

Mark is trying to go legitimate now and leave all the gangster stuff behind. He's going to college and has even talked about becoming a drug counsellor. He's still with the woman he left me for and if she thinks the sun shines out of his ass, that's her look out.

Me, I'm a lazy bitch and I don't like to work, but I've got to find a way of making some money. And I will. But this time I'll do it on my terms. The thing is, I am bright. I have a brain.

I will go forward and I will be OK. The difference is that I won't ever try to fit my life around someone else's. From now on, whatever I do to myself is what I choose to do to myself. I feel good.

ANNA CONNELLY

If ever there was a murder that divided a community it was that of Viv Graham, one of the North-East's best known hard men. Enormously strong and powerfully built, Viv was a legend in his own lifetime. More than just muscle for hire, he came to run security in Newcastle's nightclubs as well as providing protection and running a debt-collection service. To his detractors, he was an underworld crime boss who'd served time in prison for violent assault and who ruled by fear, but those who knew him tell a very different story. To them, Viv was a gentle giant, a rough diamond who conducted himself and his business according to a vigorous moral code. His supporters insist he abhorred mindless violence, put himself out to help those weaker than himself, and took a heroic stance against drugs – a stance which eventually got him killed. The men who pumped three bullets into him at close range in a North Tyneside street on New Year's Eve 1993, have never been found, despite a wide-scale police search. Viv's fiancée at the time, Anna Connelly, is still upset by how Viv was portrayed in the media follow-ing his death and agreed to appear in this book, despite her objections to its title, only in the hope of setting the record straight. Now a fifty-year-old grandmother of four, Anna's customary warmth and humour are strained only when she remembers those bleak days after the shooting . . .

Let's get one thing straight. I don't consider myself a gangster's wife. Despite all the rubbish that was writ-ten after Viv was killed about him being an enforcer who'd made millions from protection money, he was no gangster. Sure, he was no angel but he was a big guy with a big heart and I miss him every single day.

I first met Viv in 1987. He was on the door of a club and he chatted me up as I went in with my sisters and cousins. I told him I was married but he offered me a drink and my sister said, 'You might as well get a vodka from him.'

After that we'd go every week and he'd buy us drinks. He was nice with a big, wide smile and lovely teeth. And he was big, you know? He wasn't quite six foot, but he had a fifty-six-inch chest from working out twice a day. As soon as you got talking to him you realised he was one of those really kind and generous people, but because of his size and his job, people who didn't know him could be wary.

My marriage wasn't that good by this stage. My

husband was a roofer. I'd thought he was the person I'd be with for the rest of my life, particularly after we had children, but we'd been going through rough times. Then someone told my husband I'd been seen with Viv and even though I hadn't yet gone out with him at all, there was a big fight. A few weeks later we separated.

When Viv found out I wasn't with my husband any more, he came to see me and asked: 'Will you go out with me on your own now *without* your family?', because every other time he'd seen me before then I'd been with my sisters.

When we first met, he wasn't well known. He was just the big guy who used to ask people to leave the bar if they were causing trouble. Gradually, as he took over responsibility for running the doors in more and more places in the area, his reputation grew.

It's funny because I always used to think I'd marry a farmer. I grew up with my brother and three sisters in Daisy Hill, Newcastle where I've lived all my life. We had an ordinary upbringing but always kept animals and I thought I'd grow up, meet a farmer and have loads of horses.

But then in many ways, Viv was like a farmer. He was from the country and he loved animals. He was also very close to his family, who were lovely.

When I went out with Viv, I felt completely protected – like nothing bad would ever happen to me. He was such a gentleman. He'd pull out chairs for me to sit on, and hold doors open. And he was so good with the children – mine and his own that he had in previous relationships. No matter where he was he'd travel so he could see them every day.

I fell completely in love and we got engaged. It wasn't terribly romantic, mind – we were in Malta and he just bought me a ring. We got on so well it seemed natural we would marry one day.

Despite his fearsome reputation, Viv was never hard or nasty. In fact he used to worry that he was too soft-hearted, and truthfully he was very soft. If he ever punched a man, he'd make sure one of his friends was standing behind him to catch him when he fell. And then he'd stay with him until he came round. He didn't want to hurt anyone.

He was sometimes sent to collect debts and he'd ask these people to pretend he'd clouted them, and then he'd say, 'Please pay up or I really will have to clout you next time.'

But because of his size and his strength his name got around and that's how he came to run the security in our area.

All the things that have been said about a Geordie Mafia are ridiculous. Viv wasn't even really on the wrong side of the law. In fact the police spoke well of him. He made their job easier because he kept order in the clubs and wouldn't tolerate drugs. That's not to say he didn't have any problems with the law, but never about organised crime.

He got into a fight – just one hard man from Gateshead fighting another. That was the kind of fighting Viv understood. Because of the fight, he was sent to jail in 1989 and was there for eighteen months. I was disgusted. I gave him the engagement ring back when he went into prison, but he didn't want it. He threw it aside. I refused to go to visit him there even though the mothers of his children used to go. He even had sex with one woman when she went to visit and she got pregnant. That boy is now sixteen or seventeen.

Despite the other women visiting, Viv still wanted me to come. His mam came to see me and pleaded with me to go and see him, but I told her: 'I'm not visiting any jail.'

When he came out Viv came straight round to see me. I got such a shock. I said, 'Why are you coming round here? Go with the mams of your children. I've got children of my own to think about'. He said, 'I just want to be with you.' Then his mam and dad came round again to plead on his behalf and I gave in.

He had to make some changes, mind. He was a gambler and he used to go out all night gambling. When I objected, he started gambling during the day and stayed home at night. He also stopped seeing any other women. I made sure of that. I was completely convinced by the changes he'd made. He never left my side and we did everything together. I knew he was calling in to see his children, but there was nothing hidden between us after that stretch in prison.

Viv's security business was lucrative and we had a great lifestyle. He would buy me anything I wanted – as long as it wasn't too revealing – dresses costing hundreds of pounds. He was so generous and he loved seeing me happy.

He didn't bother what other people thought of him. He'd think nothing of nipping to town to buy me make-up or underwear. And he wouldn't just get you one lipstick, he'd get ten. My family – my sisters and brother – loved him. He was a genuinely nice man.

We started to make plans for the future and talked of moving to the countryside. My daughter had a horse, and we had dogs so it made a lot of sense. That was our long-term dream.

When the drugs scene started, things got very difficult. Viv was taking the drugs off people coming into the club and flushing them down the toilet. That's when the violence started – when he took on the dealers. But he knew he had to take control. He knew he had to keep one step ahead of the dealers. He was never scared for his safety. He never rang for company or for back-up. He really believed he was invincible – and I came to believe it too.

He was killed because of the drugs. It was a hatred

thing against him, because he took such a strong stand against drugs coming into the clubs.

In 1991, we started getting anonymous phone calls saying he was going to be shot and killed. The first time it happened, I was really scared and called the police. Viv said I shouldn't have done that, but I was terrified. After that the phone calls continued, but you know the more calls you get, the less you actually believe it's going to happen. Then gunmen came and shot the windows of the house, which really scared me and I called the police again.

Viv tried hard to find out who was responsible, but then it all went quiet again, and once more the fear wore off. We just thought nothing would harm us. Viv didn't take drugs or drink. He was phenomenally strong because he trained hard and worked out every day. It was an adrenalin rush for him. But it was also a social thing. The guys on the doors would all train together. He was a bit of a legend in the gym because of his strength. As his business grew, he didn't really have to be there in person – the doormen would ring him if there was a fight breaking out and he could be there within minutes.

At around this time, he started taking steroids, maybe it was his way of dealing with this new threat. The steroids changed his personality and made him quite a lot more aggressive and angry. He quite liked that because sometimes he felt he was too soft for the doors. He didn't have a lot of confidence in that way. At home he'd be bad-tempered because of the steroids. He wouldn't take it out on me or the kids, but he'd pull the doors off and things like that. Then the next day he'd have to replace them.

But then he developed a bad abscess in his backside in June 1992, probably from injecting steroids with a dirty needle. He nearly died. I got really mad with him and asking him why he was risking his life. I told his dad and he went completely berserk. He told him: 'You don't need them, son, you're a big lad.' After that, Viv stopped completely. He cared so much about what his mam and dad thought.

It was New Year's Eve 1993 that Viv was killed. We'd been at home with friends or visiting family most of the day. Then at around four p.m., Viv had driven his Ford Sierra to Wallsend High Street to have a drink with friends in the pub.

He rang me at five or six p.m. to ask if there had been any phone calls. I told him there had been a few where someone had hung up. He said he was going to buy some dog food and then come home. When Viv came out of the shop where he'd bought the dog food, he found his car window smashed and it was while he was peering inside that they shot him.

A witness heard someone shout 'Happy new year' and then 'BAM!' It was a Magnum that shot him. Three shots hit him – in his groin and his armpit. One bullet hit a major artery in his groin.

The first I knew of it was when one of the other door-men came rushing round to my house and said, 'Viv's been shot.' He was crying. I said, 'He couldn't be. I was just talking to him.' I had my pyjamas on as I'd been getting ready to go out. I got into my car and raced to the hospital so that I'd be there before he was. Viv arrived in the ambulance. He was still alive. He told me: 'Don't cry.'

The police said he'd be all right. I really thought he would be. Like I said, we all thought he was invincible. Then the doctor came and said: 'I'm afraid your husband is fighting for his life.'

After that, it's a daze. I don't really remember what happened next. I know that at some point they took me aside and said, 'We haven't been able to save him.'

I was in shock and on Valium for about six months. I just didn't want to live. If I hadn't had two young daughters I don't think I'd have been able to carry on.

It was so hard to take in. Viv was such a popular guy. Everyone loved him. He was the kind of man who carried bags for people and bought groceries for old ladies. He just wasn't violent – he was no angel but he never harmed anyone unless he absolutely had to. So for him to die in such a violent way was so shocking.

Even worse was the fact that no one was ever caught. Lots of different names have been put forward but no one knows who actually did it. I think the police did their best at the time but all their investigations led nowhere.

It was twelve weeks after he died before he was eventually buried. The funeral was a daze for me. When I've seen photos, it seems like there were millions of people there, but I just don't remember it. His parents were heartbroken, particularly his dad. It's a terrible thing for parents to outlive their child.

The Valium kept reality at bay for a while. If I could have kept on taking the tablets for ever and not had to face the world I would have done that, but eventually I had to stop them, for the sake of my family.

That feeling inside my heart was horrendous, the pain of it. We'd never got round to being married, but we were married in almost every sense. Of all the women he'd been with, he'd only ever lived with me. I missed him more than I thought possible.

We'd had so many hopes for the future. It was very hard to give up those dreams and move on. I kept thinking of how my life should have been, if he'd lived. I'd play songs over and over that reminded me of him, and I never wanted to go out.

I knew I had to move on, but I didn't want to. I wasn't looking to meet anyone else. I never thought I could, but eventually I hooked up with Michael, who'd known Viv well. He had four children and his wife was unwell and I offered to help. We finally got together ten years after Viv died.

I was thirty-four when Viv died. I'm fifty now, but it doesn't feel like that long ago. I still think about him every day. I talk about him with people all the time.

But I don't regret any of it. In spite of the grief I'd do it all again. I feel like it was such a pleasure and a privilege to have Viv in my life. Even reading those words back doesn't do justice to how I feel. He was just such a lovely person I can't even begin to describe how lucky I feel to have known him, and the same goes for my family. He gave us so much in every sense – our lives are so much richer for having known him.

If he'd lived I'm convinced Viv would have taken a back-seat role in his security business. After the drugs came, the police had to be much tougher. Before that, people used to come to the bars saying the police had sent them to ask Viv to sort out trouble. The drugs changed everything. He was the one standing out against them and that's why people wanted him dead.

I think there are many people today who didn't even know Viv but who regret what happened to him. After he was shot the club scene in our area got much nastier.

After Viv died, I was horrified by the things that were said about him in the press. The papers called him an enforcer and a thug and it made me so angry. People don't even consider the feelings of the families – his kids, his parents. Viv wasn't a gangster. You'd see these things in the papers, but the truth is no one from the

North-East is a gangster. The papers can just print anything they like.

It made me very angry. It made me want to set the record straight. We were very affected by the things they said about Viv.

He was just a big-hearted man who did his job and did it well and cared about people. There'll never be another one like him.

LYN McKAIG

It's hard to believe that the softly spoken, bearded man, shyly showing off his artwork on the wall of his mother's compact Worthing house, could once have been one of the world's biggest cocaine barons. Terry Barlow's girlfriend Lyn watches him with almost maternal pride as he explains his paintings in his quiet, diffident voice. Terry's criminal career ended with him being tried and imprisoned in both Spain and Italy for the same offence (importing forty kilos of cocaine). In total he was sentenced to twenty-nine years in prison, of which he actually served thirteen years in jails in Italy, Spain and finally the UK. When Lyn met him, he was out on parole. The couple now live a quiet life in the seaside town, looking after Terry's elderly mother.

Lyn, who herself grew up in children's homes and foster homes, is fifty-seven. Perfectly made up and looking younger than her years, she is nevertheless protective of her boyfriend, despite him being thirteen years older than her. Only when Terry is out of earshot does she talk about his past, confiding her belief that the long years in prison left something 'broken' in him. Pragmatic and matter-of-fact when talking about her own unhappy childhood, Lyn softens when discussing Terry and it's clear the pair are very close.

As soon as he walked into the club, I noticed him. He had the most amazing eyes, and I was hypnotised by them.

'Have you seen him?' I whispered, still staring across the room, to my daughter Clare.

She glanced over. 'Yeah, but he's with two women,' she said.

My heart sank. She was right. I'd been so wrapped up in watching the man that I hadn't noticed his companions. But still I couldn't stop looking at him, nor could I help but notice he was staring right back at me.

Suddenly one of the women looked towards me, whispered something to the guy, and started to make her way over.

Immediately, my pulse started racing. Had she seen me staring? Was she going to make a scene?

Instead, when she reached me, the woman leant in and said, 'He's not my boyfriend, you know? He's just a friend.'

I didn't know what to say, but before I could come up with anything, she'd returned to her friends and was whispering something to the man with the startling eyes.

'Clare!' I hissed suddenly. 'He's coming over here. What am I going to do?'

'Just relax,' she hissed back.

Then he was standing next to me. Taking my face in between his hands, he gazed intently into my eyes. 'Where've you been?' he asked. 'Where the fuck have *you* been?' I replied. And that was it. I was hooked – and have been ever since.

My life has been nothing if not dramatic. I come from an Irish/Jewish family, brought up in the East End. My mother's family are Jewish, father's Irish. It was a big family. Nan had seven kids and my mum had five. But Mum's family didn't like my father. He was not a very nice chap, a bit jealous. He's still alive, somewhere in Mansfield.

Dad did a lot of things to earn a living. He worked in a pots and pans factory, a Mars Bar factory. On my birth certificate it says 'cobbler'. He was pretty law-abiding, but he used to make us go down the market and sell things. He used to say, 'Don't come back until you've got five shillings.' We'd rob from other stalls so we had more to sell. We'd go down with a wheelbarrow and spread out a blanket. We'd sell electrical stuff like switches. He was very good at electrical stuff – that's where I get my knowledge from because I'm very good with electrics.

My mum died when I was ten. She had epilepsy. She was a very nervous person. I now have what she had – agoraphobia. She got to the stage where she couldn't go out at all and was having panic attacks. She kept trying to kill herself. I'd come home from school and her head would be in the oven. In the end she had an epileptic fit from a blow to the head. She died in 1961.

I had one sister and three brothers. My dad brought his sister-in-law, who was living in Mansfield, to live with us. She was married to my dad's twin brother but he'd died from a war wound. She came over with her two children, both girls. So there were four girls and three boys. The house was too crowded and Dad fussed over them such a lot we felt we didn't fit in. In the end, we sat down together and said that we wanted to go into care. We'd been in and out of care before as respite for Mum. We told them we wanted to go back there.

I never lived with my father again. Until recently I kept in touch with him but then he started running Mum down so I don't bother any more. I told his wife to take my name out of their address book. I went into care in Hornchurch in Essex. There were houses all called by names of flowers – like Rose Cottage. Now I think it's a girls' school, but then it was a children's home, after that I went to Barnardo's.

After a few years my aunt, my mum's younger sister, took me in, and my nan had my sister, and my brothers went to my uncle. I didn't get on with my aunt, whose two children I looked after. Eventually I got taken away from her suffering from malnutrition.

My schoolteacher, Joanne Barlow, had noticed me coming to school in the snow with no coat, and she befriended me and looked after me. Then social services came and got me and I went back into care. Then, when I was twelve, I went to stay with Joanna. Now I think it's funny that her name was Barlow and so is Terry's. It's like a good omen.

Joanne was very good to me, but she'd already applied to be a missionary in Nigeria so when she went away, I went to live with another couple. They were fine, but then we had to go to stay with the husband's father who was ill. He was a nasty old man and sexually abused me. They thought I was ungrateful because every time he was around I'd be rude to him. I was about fourteen. I ran away and went back into care.

When Joanna found out what had happened, I went to stay with her sister Kate in Buckinghamshire. So you could say I'd had a bit of a rootless upbringing. Certainly by the time I'd left school at fourteen I'd experienced a lot more than I should have done.

At eighteen I got married to Keith and had my son Gary, who's thirty-eight. It's common among kids who grew up in care to have children early – I suppose it's a desire to create the family they missed out on. I was far too young, I wasn't ready. I knew how to defend myself but I was immature emotionally.

Keith was a good provider, a carpenter. We lived near Bletchley in what's now called Milton Keynes. Three years later I had Clare. I've now got three grandchildren, including a seventeen-year-old. Keith and I were together twelve years before we got divorced. I was running a pub in Haywards Heath at the time. After that I had two long-term love affairs, but neither of them came to anything.

By the time the new millennium came round, I was living in a flat in Worthing and was really depressed and tired with it all. I felt like my life had been full of failures. I stopped going out altogether.

One day in 2001, my daughter rang me. She said, 'You can't keep sitting in the flat night after night, you've got to go out.' I said, 'I don't want to.' She said, 'I'm driving down now, I'm going to pick you up and we're going out.'

There's a pub near here with a nightclub attached. Clare insisted we were going there. I really didn't want to go. At forty-nine, I felt I'd be the oldest person there.

She dragged me into the pub for a drink to get my nerve up, then we went to the nightclub. I was standing there feeling very self-conscious, but then I saw the man with the fantastic eyes coming in. I found out later Terry had been on E when he came over and took my face in his hands. I was so naive, I didn't even know what E was.

'What's an E?' I asked.

He said, 'It's Ecstasy.' I said, 'What's Ecstasy?' He said, 'Never mind.'

When I met him in the nightclub it was a Wednesday night. We didn't really talk much but he said, 'Let's meet up for a coffee on Friday.' 'Friday?' I said. 'What's wrong with tomorrow?'

So we met the next day. I was with my daughter and granddaughter. I said, 'Go round the corner and have a look, see if he's there, and tell me if he looks as nice as last night.' She went to look and said, 'He's there.'

We talked and talked. I couldn't believe he was sixty-two. He dropped a few hints that he might have some big secret in his past. He told me that I might not want to go out with him if he told me everything. I kept saying that nothing he said could shock me.

He eventually came out with it all about three weeks later. We'd been seeing each other every day and I think he was frightened about my reaction if I found out from someone else. As he was telling me, I was looking at him and thinking: You're having me on, you're not that sort of person. Then he showed me his legal papers – translated into different languages, and I knew it was true.

Terry had been done for big-time cocaine smuggling. He'd been sentenced to twenty-nine years in prison, and had actually served thirteen. He'd known all the big people, like Pablo Escobar. He was right up there.

He made an awful lot of money. He lived in America

with his wife and they lived the high life with his daughter and sons. Nice house, boat, cars. But he'd got so big, he was running around like a headless chicken and by the time he was caught I think it was almost a relief.

I've seen a picture of Terry and his wife together. She'd hurt her eye and has a patch over it. They look like Bonnie and Clyde. Terry was always having to go on the run from the Colombian mafia. One time Terry even went on the run with his mum. She'd come over to see him and then all of a sudden he was saying: 'Right, Mum, pack your bags, you're coming with me.' Another time he was on the run with his daughter. He'd run while they were looking for him then come back when the heat was off.

His whole life was a comedy. He was way out of his depth. One time he was waiting for these guys to come to give him money. He was getting more and more anxious because they were late. All of a sudden the door flew open and out of sheer fright he grabbed a gun and the guys were terrified and screamed, 'We'll pay you we'll pay you.' Obviously Terry looked like this hard guy, but the truth was he was more scared than they were. It was funny. There were loads of mistakes, but he still made loads of money.

He was eventually arrested in Italy. Terry went to prison because this guy he worked with blabbed to save his own skin. He's the one who brought Terry down. I could wring his neck. And he owes Terry money. We're still looking for him.

All Terry's money was taken when he was arrested, all the Swiss bank accounts were frozen. He has no idea exactly how much money he used to have, but let's just say he used to weigh it rather than count it.

He paid loads of money out in solicitors' fees to try to get his case heard early, but it was a very corrupt system and someone else was paying for his papers to keep being put to the bottom of the pile the whole time.

I think Terry was pretty broken by his prison experience. Thirteen years is a lifetime in prison. He was in prison in Italy, Spain and then the UK, ending up in Wandsworth. He missed his daughter and his sons terribly, but they were in the US and couldn't visit.

Prison obviously changed him. Before, he was a Jack the Lad, a very good-looking man, the sort of guy who'd wear a jacket and roll the sleeves up. He's like the character in *Blow*. In fact his wife rang him up when she'd seen the film and said, 'How dare you sell our story.' The only good thing about prison was he really got into art. He ended up teaching it, and doing murals. That's what kept him sane, I think.

When I met Terry, he'd been out of prison for six months and had lost all his confidence. He was living first with his mum and then in a kind of halfway house that was full of drug addicts. That's who gave him an

E the night we met – otherwise he'd never have had the confidence to venture out.

I was in his flat one day and opened the drawer and there was this big block of something. I said, 'What's that?' He said, 'It's resin. I'm looking after it for someone.' I couldn't believe it. I said, 'Get it out *now*. That's all you need, for them to come and search this place and find that.'

When Terry told me the truth about his past, three weeks into our relationship, I was really surprised. By that stage I'd worked out it was something criminal, but I had no idea it was that big. To be honest, it didn't really put me off him. In fact it was quite exciting in a way. But I was frustrated about how stupid he'd been. I don't mean stupid to do it in the first place, I mean stupid to get caught! As he was telling me, I kept thinking: Why did you do it like that, instead of like this?

After that, it did cross my mind that I should walk away instead of getting more involved, but I really liked him.

I told him that I'd never broken the law in my life, except for stealing off the market stalls and when I was younger and in care. We used to nick little things like balls of mohair wool and hide them under the mattress, then when we had to turn the mattresses over, which we did every few days, I got into trouble. Bed at six o'clock for about a month and no pocket money.

Really, being in care was like being in prison so I

suppose Terry and I had that in common. I made the decision to stay with him, and we became inseparable.

I think if Terry hadn't met me, he would have got back into the drugs thing because it was all he knew. At one point he went off looking at boats in Shoreham. I said, 'What are you looking at boats for?' Really, I knew exactly what he was doing that for and so I said, 'If you go back to what you were doing before, I'm not going to stick around.'

I wasn't making a moral judgement but I thought he'd been through enough. He hadn't been that clever the first time, but somehow he'd managed to get away with it for a long time, but I felt his luck had run out. If you're going to do something like that, you've got to be very clever. There are people out there who don't keep things to themselves. One night we had a big row about it. I stomped off to my own flat – that was the only night I ever spent on my own since we met.

I knew right from the beginning that Terry and I would stay together. I don't really know why. I'm a bit of a control freak; I like the idea that I keep Terry on the straight and narrow. I feel I've won. I was always nosy about what he was doing, making sure he didn't get up to anything.

I was very protective of Terry in a way. The people he lived with in the flats used to call him The Don, but they were taking the piss out of him. One time they didn't tell him that a seagull had pooped in his chips and they were just laughing at him. I was furious. I thought: 'how dare you?

It's funny, I suppose, me trying to protect this big-time cocaine smuggler, but that's the way it has been. Terry has said to me that he thinks he'd probably be back inside if it wasn't for me.

Mind you, you never completely escape the past, do you? Most of the people he knew before are either inside or dead but a few of the ones in prison have kept in touch with him.

When I was first living with him, some guys came and knocked on the door wanting him to be a witness in a court case in Italy. Terry was still on parole and told them he couldn't come over. He said he didn't have a passport, even though he did. He just didn't want to get a reputation as a snitch.

Since we've been together he has been rebuilding his relationship with his children back in America. His daughter came over to see him with her husband and he hadn't seen her since she was ten. It was very emotional.

He's got two sons. One is posted over in Iraq. The other is doing really well building houses in Massachusetts. Has his own construction company. He says, 'I always remember what you said to me, Dad: you told me you'll never make any money working for someone else.' That's one good thing Terry did.

The life Terry lived before prison was completely

outside of my experience, but that doesn't really scare me. I'm not a softie by any means. You've got to cover yourself in this world, nobody else is going to look after you. If I had felt Terry was somehow a threat to me or my way of life, I'd be up and gone. I know Terry used to dabble in drugs, but he was never an addict. He says he used to look at people taking it and think: You're talking crap. Two days could go just taking line after line and talking rubbish.

We live in a little house in Worthing now with Terry's mum. Sometimes when I think about his past, and the money he used to have, I do have those feelings of 'I wish I'd known him then'. It's the worst thing in the world knowing there's all that money sitting frozen in Swiss bank accounts and not being able to get it. And of course, if I'd known him then, I'd have made sure he never got caught!

But, to be honest, I don't think we'd have got on in those days. He was a shopaholic. Everything was designer this and that. He was so abuzz with it, he wasn't such a good person. So it's probably quite good we didn't meet then. Mind you, I think I would have been all right on the run. I've always run away. My whole life has been running away.

I don't want to do any more running. I've found what I was looking for at long last.

BECKY LOY

After nearly three decades of conventional, but unfulfilling marriage in the Midlands, Becky Loy was desperate for adventure. Sometimes, as they say, you should be careful what you wish for. Newly divorced, she moved to southern Spain and almost immediately hooked up with Alex, a Romanian gangster, twenty-two years her junior. Alex had been in and out of prison as a youngster, mostly for car theft, and had graduated to drug deals on the Costa del Sol.

Always volatile and macho, Alex's behaviour grew increasingly erratic as he became dependent on steroids. The relationship cracked just as quickly as Becky's finances crumbled, with Alex eventually going back to live in Romania where he has been for the last two years.

Now fifty-nine, Becky faces getting older without either financial or emotional support. A tough, un-self-pitying woman, her heavily mascaraed eyes nevertheless brim over when describing how she's had to scrabble around to survive over the last years, even resorting to being a high-class dominatrix to try to make a living. However, she prides herself on being a survivor and, despite everything, remains fondly indulgent towards her errant Romanian husband.

When we meet, she is trapped in a nightmare domestic set-up, the fledgling property consultancy she is trying to set up has just been evicted from its offices and she is down to her last twenty-five euros, but she insists she is optimistic about the future. I leave her sitting at a plastic café table on a busy thoroughfare in Fuengirola, making calls on her mobile phone, trying to sort out yet another deal to get her out of her current crisis – still determined to see it as the next step in her great adventure.

I thought it was a bit strange when my new husband Alex asked me to stop the car suddenly. We'd been out for a long drive and were on our way home when he directed me through a neighbourhood I'd never been in before.

'Stay here,' he told me. 'I'll be back soon.'

He was always disappearing and I'd learned not to ask too many questions. 'Everything OK?' I asked when he got back.

'Fine,' he said, not meeting my eyes and fidgeting with something by his feet.

As we arrived back at our apartment, he slid a carrier bag out from under the seat.

'What's that?' I asked, suspiciously.

'Nothing,' he replied, but I could see from his face that it was far from nothing.

'Show me,' I insisted.

Inside the bag was a gun and what looked like big bars of chocolate.

I shrieked at him to get rid of the gun. 'What are you doing bringing that into my car?' I yelled. 'And why have you got bars of chocolate?'

That's how naive I was. I didn't even know those were bars of hashish. I'm telling you, when you marry a gangster, you learn fast.

But then nothing about my early years had prepared me for meeting someone like Alex.

I came from the Midlands. I married young to a fabulous guy and we had a son together, but I always had a business head on me. At first I had a nursing home in Birmingham, then when I sold that, we moved out towards Stratford-upon-Avon and I worked in a hotel near the theatre. I liked that because I met a lot of nice people. Then I ended up going to work for the Hilton group of hotels.

My husband and I enjoyed a good standard of living, but it wasn't an exciting life. He was a good man, but he was boring. We'd stopped having sex quite early on.

For sixteen years I didn't so much as kiss a guy. I used to think to myself: Surely I was destined for more than that? As it turned out, I was right – though not quite in the way I envisaged.

The first change came when I started an affair with a guy I'd known for five years. I didn't set out for it to happen but once it did, it was as though I'd been woken up to life. When that guy moved to Australia I really missed that feeling of being alive. I missed the sex.

A friend of mine said, 'You've not been happy for years. Why don't you get yourself an escort?'

It may sound extreme, but I was at a really restless stage. I'd had skin cancer, undergone a hysterectomy and my mum died at the age of fifty-six, so there was a bit of me going 'hang on, I only get one shot at all of this'.

So I contacted an escort agency. Chris and I hit it off straight away. That first 'date' led to a second and then a third, and then we were seeing each other regularly. It was easy to hide it from my husband. We'd always had separate bank accounts and we didn't keep an eye on each other's money. The absences weren't hard to explain: I was on a nursing course, or I was out with the girls.

When my escort asked if I'd ever skied (he was foreign and was practically born on skis) I said, 'Let's go for it.' We went skiing, we went on holidays together. It went on for three years and cost me a fortune. I think I spent over £60,000 on Chris over the years, although I didn't pay every single time we were together. In all that time my husband never clicked. I certainly didn't want to hurt him.

Inevitably, being with Chris made me increasingly dissatisfied with my marriage. One day my husband and I were arguing and he said, 'Well, why don't you get a divorce if you're not happy?' and I said, 'OK, I will.' And that was that. We were together twenty-seven years and I couldn't fault the guy, but he was just the wrong husband for me.

The problem was that I fell in love with Chris. That may sound naive considering I was paying him to be with me, but it actually turned into a good relationship in many ways. When I was ill he was there for me. It wasn't all one-sided. Still, I knew it wasn't going anywhere and began looking at ways to make a clean break and start again.

After the divorce I was quite well off. I went out to southern Spain, which I'd fallen in love with some time before, and put a deposit on an investment property. Back in England, I started talking to a group of girl-friends. We were all a bit disenchanted with life, and I said, 'I've got a property in Spain, I've got a bit of money. Let's open a bar.'

So I flew back to Spain to do a bit of research, then went back again, and that was it really. It was very quick – everything was sorted within a month.

Coming over to Spain was part running away and part wanting to start a new life. I had no intentions of another fella – not immediately anyway. Everything just seemed right for a move. My escort had taught me that there was more to life than just trundling along in a boring rut, waiting to draw my pension. I felt it was a case of now or never.

Chris helped me with the move. We drove over together in October 1999 with a car full of stuff and found an apartment in a coastal resort called Duquesa. Then as my two girlfriends flew in, he flew out, literally crossing at the airport.

And that was it. We went round a few agents, looking at clubs, found what we wanted and put a deposit down. By that time it was Christmas.

Duquesa is a very enclosed port so everyone knows everybody. They all thought we were dykes to start with because we were always together – one Australian woman and two English. We were the talk of the town – mind you, people down there get excited about a Tupperware party, so it wasn't saying much.

We'd been invited to a friend's bar on Christmas night. When we got there it was closed. By this time we were already well oiled. We thought: It's Christmas. We have to go out. We heard this disco music coming from the port and followed it. It was a private function and we were really casually dressed in jeans, but they invited us. We danced about. Then these four guys came in. My girlfriend immediately fancied one of them, who turned out to be Brazilian, but my attention was on his dark, handsome friend.

My girlfriend got chatted up by the Brazilian. They wanted to fix up a date for the following night but she didn't speak any Spanish and he didn't speak any English. I spoke a little bit of Spanish, so they introduced me to the friend, whose name was Alex and who seemed to speak every language under the sun, to get the exchange of telephone numbers done. There wasn't very much contact between us that night, but there was something about him I found really attractive, although I could tell he was a lot younger than me.

The next day my friend asked me to come with her in case her date didn't show up. So we both got all dolled up and Alex came along, doing a double take when he saw us. He told us his friend would be along shortly and sat down next to me, looked into my eyes and that really was it. It was instant.

All that night we chatted as if we were the only two people in the room. He was very charismatic, very attentive. He made me feel special. He's a fabulous dancer and I love dancing and I was impressed by the fact he could speak seven languages.

We started seeing each other. I thought he was Italian at first. He played a little game with me. He spoke Italian most of the time with some French. It wasn't until three months later, when he was about to move into my apartment, that I found out the truth – that he was actually Romanian and that he'd spent seven years in prisons in three different countries, mostly for car theft.

I took that in my stride. 'I've got a confession as well,' I told him. 'I'm not forty-one, I'm forty-nine.' He said, 'I know. I've already looked at your passport.' Then he revealed he was twenty-seven, not thirty-six as he'd told me.

Funnily enough, the twenty-two-year age gap didn't seem to be an obstacle. We liked the same things. I loved trying to talk to him in French, which I'd studied at school, and he was a fabulous cook. He loved music and opera. I got a piano and tried to teach him to play. We spent every day together.

When my friends found out Alex was Romanian, I had to take an awful lot of flak because Romanians cause an awful lot of problems over here – but then so do English, so do Moroccans, so do Arabs. One person does not represent a country.

From early on, I knew he'd been in trouble with the law in the past. He didn't hold back what he'd done. I knew he'd been a drug dealer. Because he told me about his childhood, I could see why he did it. He was kicked out of the house at fourteen, dropped in Germany, and told to get on with life. No kid of fourteen can survive living on the streets without meeting the wrong people.

At first I thought the drug dealing was all in the past

but when we started living together, I realised it wasn't. He was very secretive. He'd say, 'Oh, I'm going out. I'll be back at eleven or twelve.' It would get to one o'clock, two o'clock, three o'clock and he'd still not be back. Then I'd get a phone call to let him in the apartment. He'd never say where he'd been, but I knew there was something dodgy going on. There were organised gangs dealing in drugs along the coast, and I realised he was probably involved with one of those.

I told him I didn't want him doing it. But in the end, what could I do? I had to accept it. And besides, he could be so romantic I forgot about everything else. He'd go off and disappear and I wouldn't know where he was and then on his way back he'd call in at the garage and buy a little teddy bear or a rose.

I pinned my hopes on the club I was setting up with my friends. We were rushing around getting staff contracts drawn up. I was going to get Alex to provide the security. It was going to be an ideal new start for him, his chance to do a normal job, which he'd never done before. It would take a total change of mindset.

At the same time though, I was worrying privately about whether Alex was with me because he thought I had money. Let's face it, that's what most people think if they see a young guy with a much older woman. I know I fell in love with him quicker than he fell in love with me, and the imbalance bothered me. It was always in the back of my mind.

Then something happened that really put his true feelings to the test. When Alex and I had been together a few months, the arrangements for the nightclub I'd planned to open were finally sorted. I phoned my divorce mediator in England who'd been holding the money from my settlement in trust and left a message saying: 'Right, everything's ready to go. Can you transfer the money from my account now?' I should have heard alarm bells when he never rang back. Finally I spoke to him and he told me he needed to come over to Spain to check everything was in order.

I thought it was a bit strange, but it was a lot of money and I assumed he had a duty of care to make sure the divorce settlement wasn't going to be wasted on a precarious venture.

When the mediator arrived, he didn't actually seem that interested in the club but was much more concerned with talking to me about his own company and trying to persuade me to invest in that instead or as well. I said, 'My life is in Spain now. I don't want to invest in a company in England'. He seemed disappointed but resigned and promised to transfer the money as soon as he arrived back in the UK.

But once he'd got back, I couldn't get him on the phone. I left message after message and got no reply. Also, no money. Increasingly concerned, I contacted a lawyer in England and then the fraud squad. To cut a long story short I never got the money and I lost the club. There was a two-year court case but no one could recover the money.

After that, my whole life collapsed like a pack of cards. I lost my investment home in Spain because I had to sell that to survive. I couldn't pay the mortgage on my property in England so I lost that. In total I lost £450,000. That was my entire life savings, including my divorce settlement.

From being a relatively wealthy woman, I was now penniless. I was fifty years old and I had no home, no business and no prospects.

If Alex had been after my money, he'd have been out of there like a shot, but he stuck by me. Even when we ended up living in the car for a little while, he didn't leave me. That's when I finally accepted he loved me for me, not for what he thought I could give him.

We both did whatever work we could do to get back on our feet a little. Then, while the court case was going on, I went over to Romania to meet Alex's family. At the time people told me I was mad to go to Romania – I'd be taken off and never heard from again. In fact it was the opposite. When I arrived at the airport, the security guards took my bags. I was like royalty. Alex had gone on ahead of me and when I arrived, he was stood there and he kissed my hand – which was the Romanian way. We couldn't cuddle in front of anybody. I just melted.

The poverty in Romania shocked me. I had never been anywhere with no running water or electricity and you went outside to do your business in a hole in the ground. People were getting up at five a.m. to go to work in a horse and cart. It was an eye-opener, seeing kids with deformed limbs.

Alex's aunt ran a children's hospital. When I first visited, I thought: Oh my God, we've got to do something to help. We even went as far as setting up a registered charity, although we've never had enough money to get it off the ground.

The first Christmas we were there, we went to the hypermarket and I spent a load of money and we made all these parcels and delivered them out to outlying villagers where we knew the father wasn't there and there was no money for Christmas. That was the best Christmas I ever had. That's what Christmas is supposed to be like.

Even though she's a year younger than me, I got on famously with Alex's mum. She said, 'If my Alex is happy, I'm happy.' The whole family made me feel very welcome.

That's not to say it was all perfect. Alex has a terrible temper and that first visit to Romania showed a violent side to him. When I arrived, he'd hired a friend to drive us around. The friend kept coming on to me and Alex saw it. He lashed out and caught me with his ring and cut my eye open. I got out of the car and just ran.

He ran after me and he was sobbing his heart out. He said, 'I'm so sorry.' I said, 'What happened?' That's when I realised that all the beatings he'd suffered as a child had taken their toll. I think he thought I was just going to go off with this other guy.

He said, 'I don't want you to leave. I'm in love with you.' I forgave him of course, but I was worried this would turn out not to be a one-off – and I was right.

Meanwhile I got back in touch with my ex-husband. He knew what had happened with the divorce settlement and obviously felt sorry for me. We'd had a home in Florida and I asked if he'd consider selling it. He said, 'Well, I'm never going to go there because there are too many memories.' So he sold that and sent the money over to me. That was a financial lifeline.

Alex and I decided to set up a hairdressing salon in his city in Romania. There was only one salon in the whole of the city so there was plenty of scope. That was going to be another new start. Alex was so excited, I felt it could really turn his life around. Away from the organised gangs back in the Costa del Sol, he could throw himself into something legitimate.

The initial arrangements all went well and I left Alex in charge of sorting things out in Romania while I flew back and forth to Spain trying to earn what money I could, working mostly for telesales companies or property developers.

On one of my visits back to Romania, Alex proposed.

I got in the car at the airport and he said, 'We get married.' I said, 'OK.' He had the ring already, so I put it on. It wasn't the most romantic thing, but that was him all over.

I didn't have any doubts about the marriage, although that's partly because some Romanian marriages are symbolic and don't count anywhere else. There were no legal documents. We had a ceremony in Alex's mother's house with a proper priest but it was more of a blessing than a proper marriage.

The day was lovely. His mother did it the English way. We weren't allowed to see each other the night before. He stayed in her house, I stayed in an apartment. In the morning I was told I had to stay in the bedroom of the house and get prepared. I could hear people coming in and furniture being moved. I'd bought a long gold Chinese-style dress. I got all ready and was summoned out. When I came out there were garlands of flowers everywhere and candles and lots of tables of food and the priest was there along with the family and other guests. All the women were in long dresses. It was just lovely – I'd never been happier in my life.

Some guests at that wedding may have wondered about the age gap, but to tell you the truth it bothered me far more than him. He always told me he'd never particularly liked young girls. He's got a very low opinion of younger girls because the ones he knows either have worked as prostitutes or at least got paid for sex. In Romania they'd do a blow job for five euros to get some money to get a driving lesson.

After about nine months of hard work, the salon opened. I invited a hairdressing friend of mine to fly over to do a celebrity masterclass. Everyone adored him and we had a really busy week and there was champagne for all the new clients and it all looked like it was going to go really well.

Alex was in his element, and once again I left him at the helm while I flew back to Spain to work. Big mistake. I don't know what got into his head. He decided he was a businessman and didn't need to ask me anything. He totally ruined the business. He borrowed some money against it and extended it and bought extra land. He thought he was doing the right thing by expanding. But while it might have been the right thing eventually, to do it so soon was a catastrophic mistake.

Plus, he'd borrowed it from the wrong people. The salon was never going to start generating the kind of returns we needed so soon after starting, so the bit of money we had left we had to use to pay the loan off, leaving us nothing to run the business.

It all got very fraught, and I was frightened because of how violent things can get there. I remember one time Alex had a phone call and within ten minutes five cars had arrived full of blokes. I said, 'What are you doing?' He said, 'Now we do boom boom.' They'd all arranged to meet up and have a big fight. I couldn't believe it.

Despite our best efforts, we ended up hopelessly over-stretched and we lost the salon – and with it the last of my financial security. I was back at square one – broke and homeless, utterly demoralised and furious with Alex.

While the loss of the business didn't split us up, it inevitably caused a lot of friction between us. Alex felt humiliated and, as he's such a proud person, that made him defensive and angry. I was hugely resentful. I realised that I was basically on my own, and the only person I could rely on was myself.

Desperate for money, I was introduced to a guy who lives over here in Spain – I can't say much about him because he's well known – who was into bondage. He's rich and offered me a job working for him as a high-class dominatrix. He offered to set me up in a villa and assured me I wouldn't have to have sex with the clients as there were two other girls who took care of all of that. I'd just have to 'discipline' them.

It was such a world away from the life I'd lived up until that point, but I was really desperate. We had no money, nowhere to live. When he said Alex could provide the security, I thought: What have I got to lose?

Actually the dominatrix work wasn't as bad as I'd feared. It's pure escapism. You put on the costume and the make-up and you become someone else. Even though I didn't have sex with the clients, it was very hard for Alex to accept me doing that kind of work. It really got to him. But there really was no alternative. I lived in the villa and he stayed in an apartment I'd rented, but most of the time I couldn't even afford the electricity.

Because there was an interdiction order against him, Alex kept having to go back to Romania for three months at a time. I really missed him when he was gone. One time I even flew him back to Spain on his brother's passport, just to see him. Ironically, he was completely clean while he was in Romania. You don't do those kinds of crimes there unless you want to go to prison for twenty-five years.

When he came back to Spain we moved back in together and while I was working at anything to make money, he soon fell back in with the gang. Most of the time he was involved in drugs. He'd never carry drugs. He'd be involved in the transport. He was very careful. He never wanted to do really big deals, although he wanted the big money. He acted really big, but inside there was a lot of scared little boy.

Our relationship started changing. He'd always had a violent temper but it became more and more out of control. One minute we'd be having the most fantastic time, and the next he completely lost it – mostly about money. Things got so bad that I paid for him to have brain scans done and it turns out he actually has what's known as Intermittent Explosive Disorder – a malfunction of the brain that can lead to impulsive outbursts of anger. That's from damage he's had before.

Through reading up about it, I learned to recognise the trigger – the telltale sign that he's about to get violent. He'd start repeating a phrase over and over again and then his mind would go black and he'd have no idea what was happening to him or what he was saying or doing. So as soon as he started repeating himself I learned to get out of the way.

But when things were good with Alex, they were very very good. He was much like my escort in many ways. He could make me feel a million dollars. When we went out to clubs I loved to see the jealousy on other women's faces and to think: Hands off. He's mine. While the relationship was volatile, it was also very romantic. The sex was good, and I loved the fact that he was a good-looking guy. I wanted to be seen with him, I felt safe with him, I felt protected.

And he did really love me in his own way. I was badly ill once and he carried me to the car, took me to the hospital, grabbed a doctor by the scruff of the neck and said, 'My wife is sick. You come now. She's priority.' That's when I felt loved. He sat by my bed for five days and five nights and didn't move.

The problem is, you never feel secure with a gangster. If Alex disappeared for three or four days, I'd convince myself he wasn't coming back. His phone would be off and it would feed my insecurities. Every year I was getting older. Him disappearing would leave me feeling neglected and deserted. I'd had a difficult childhood – I'd been deserted by my father and had been abused. I don't care what people say, it doesn't matter how good your therapy is, that kind of experience leaves scars. So both Alex and I had scars and sometimes those scars just opened up and all the shit would come back.

But while I kept trying to understand him, he couldn't always understand me. He couldn't understand how my childhood sometimes made me react badly towards him, and tempers would become frayed. It was a case of a couple of very peculiar people coming together.

Sometimes when he disappeared, I'd think there must be another woman. Because our sex life was quite active, I didn't know how he could cope without sex while he was gone. I'd torture myself by imagining him with a gang of guys who all decided to go to a whorehouse. How would he be able to say no?

The only thing that slightly reassured me was that he was absolutely obsessive about cleanliness and paranoid about AIDS. I think that comes from living on the streets and being in prison.

Money was a constant source of friction. I was working at anything to get money. There used to be a lot of scams operating on the Costa del Sol, mostly to do with timeshare, and I was guilty of working them without knowing. We all do these jobs unwittingly and then discover they're scams. You either don't know or you don't ask. At the end of the day, everyone has to have a roof over their heads and food on the table. You do what you do to survive over here. It's dog eat dog. I call it the Costa del Bullshit. If I had a hundred Kalashnikovs full of bullets, it wouldn't be enough to wipe out all the twats over here.

Out of desperation I went back to live with the guy who'd turned me into the dominatrix. It's a complicated arrangement I don't really want to go into, but Alex was left on his own in a studio apartment, which he hated. That was about three years ago, and Alex and I have never had a home together since. It was really difficult for him, especially when the money ran out and I couldn't pay the utilities so he had no electricity and no hot water. We were just spending probably an hour together once a week and it was getting to him.

The illegal stuff started to dry up. Alex had been quite a big boy down here, he was well respected in criminal circles. Although he was young, they knew that if he said he could do something, it would be organised and it would go without a hitch. They never ever got caught so they knew he was a good organiser and they knew everyone around him could be trusted and there wouldn't be problems, and no one would dob them in.

But gradually it all started to change. Nowadays you

don't know who's who any more. The police are a lot sharper, they infiltrate the gangs. People who have problems with the police turn informant to get a reduced prison sentence. The fraud squad have opened up an office in Málaga and are trying to close down all the scams, which is good. It's about bloody time.

Alex became increasingly isolated and frustrated as he struggled to find anything to do – legal or otherwise. He started getting very aggressive and was spending long hours at the gym. I didn't know it at the time, but he was getting hooked on steroids which were radically affecting his personality.

One day we had an almighty bust-up. I found out he'd got some money and he never told me. He finally admitted he'd done a job for someone but hadn't wanted to tell me in case I was angry. He wouldn't tell me what it was and, to be honest, I didn't want to know. I was upset because he didn't offer me any money, and I needed it at the time.

We were at this pizza restaurant we always went to and we had a big row and Alex threw the tables and chairs around. I really shouted at him, yelling, 'You've got to get away. I don't want to know you. It's over.' He disappeared and this time I didn't even try to find him. I was too angry. The next thing I knew I had a phone call from Romania. Alex was there and he'd lost the use of his arm.

That's when I discovered Alex had been abusing

steroids while he was in Spain. Then when he went back to Romania and couldn't get hold of them any more, he'd had an almighty reaction. They didn't know whether it was a brain tumour, a stroke or what. So I borrowed some money and got him into hospital over there and I haven't seen him since although we talk twice a day. He's out of hospital now and his arm is almost recovered, but he's still over in Romania.

As for me, I'm still living with the guy in the villa, but it's not a good situation. He's a control freak and, it also turns out, a Satanist. If ever I mention God he always says, 'What has HE ever done for you?' I don't know if I can stay there much longer, but I don't have anywhere else to go. It's scary.

But I'm a survivor, and I'm philosophical. I'm one of those people who believes you have to go through certain things to get to the right place. I believe something will come along eventually. Maybe this stage is a bit of comeuppance. I did have a very good life in the UK and I wasted a lot of money. I could go out with £500 in my pocket and not worry about it. Maybe this is payback time.

Mind you, I don't regret the divorce and I certainly don't regret meeting Alex. It's almost as though we were fated. I still believe we were destined to meet and destined to go through all this.

One time I asked him what he thought when he first met me. He said, 'You know when you do camera with a special light and it goes "boom"? The first time I saw you, something in my head went "boom" because I could see your soul was good.' He always says to me my soul is good. I know I have got a good soul although I'm not always easy to live with. Equally I know his soul is good. He may have a terrible temper, but his heart is as big as the world.

If I'm honest, I'd like Alex to do just one more job – a big one just to get us back on our feet. I'm scared of the future. I'm fifty-nine years old and I haven't got a penny. Can I go on indefinitely working twelve hours a day doing two jobs?

But I know that big job is not going to happen. Alex just won't do the really big stuff. He'll do 'B' but not 'A' or 'C'. I think his time in prison scared him too much.

I still love Alex, absolutely. And I still feel married to him. I'd love for us to be together again. If I made money again he'd come over. I've got friends with nightclubs who'd give him a job. If not, maybe we'd get a bit of money together and go to England. You take every day as it comes over here. You take every minute as it comes.

I don't know where our relationship will go. I don't know if we'll end up staying together. He says he wants to stay with me. He says, 'I don't care if you're in a wheelchair, I don't care if I have to feed you, I don't care if you do- -pee in the bed. I want to be with you.' I do know at one point in his life he was with a woman who got cancer and he stayed with her through to the bitter end, so I think he's probably telling the truth.

It's a loving relationship, but it's a long-distance one and it's easy to have a relationship over the phone. I'm very independent. I like my own space now. If we do get back together it's not going to be easy. There'll have to be a lot of adapting.

I'll always love Alex, but whether or not I can cope with living with him permanently again, I don't know. It's no good me saying that it's all going to be lovey dovey. Sure, we might go out to a club and have a dance or a lovely meal. But I like to get up in the morning and have a cigarette; he likes to get up and have his coffee and his crap and *then* he has a cigarette. Little things like that can cause friction.

Alex doesn't really understand how dire things are financially for me. He thinks I can do anything. Sometimes he puts too much pressure on me and I can't do it and then he thinks I've let him down. He rang me up the other day and said he'd found land ideal for a golf course, and asked me to find someone here to finance it. I said, 'Where am I going to find someone with that sort of money?' He said, 'Of course you can. There are loads of people with money there. You find one.'

Because of his gangster past, he thinks he can just

snap his fingers and things will come to him. Because that's how it used to happen for him. If he wanted something, he'd rob it and if he had to take money from a prostitute who'd worked all night, he'd do it. His philosophy is you do what you need to survive.

I'm often tempted to go back to England. My son, who's twenty-eight, has had a child so I'm a grandmother now, although my son and I don't always see eye to eye. I've got a job waiting for me in the UK as a PA to a friend of mine who's got his own business, but he wants more than just a working relationship and I don't. I'm still married to Alex. I've never even so much as kissed another man.

I try to stay positive because you never know what's around the corner. You don't know what tomorrow might bring. You just have to live for today. If you can't eat one day, you don't eat one day. If you do you do. It's how most of the world lives. I'm no different to millions of others.

What disappoints me is that Alex and I wanted to improve life for Romanian children. When I went round that hospital I just wanted to get my nurse's uniform on again and help them.

And Alex has got that sort of heart too. We're destined to do something together. God knows what it is. We might do something fantastic, or we might kill each other. The way my life is at the moment, nothing would surprise me.

FLANAGAN

Ask anyone to name a quintessential gangster, and they'll probably say the Krays – the iconic twin brothers who ruled the East End in the 1960s with threats and violence. Ask that same person to picture the quintessential gangster's moll, and they'll probably describe someone like Maureen Flanagan. Now sixty-eight, but still oozing glamour from the top of her peroxide blonde hair to her perfectly painted toenails, Flanagan (as she is universally known) was a child of her time. During the 1960s, as the Krays built their empire, setting up nightclubs and protection rackets, Flanagan was a top model, zipping around London in her Mini, trademark long blonde hair flying behind her, wearing hot pants and knee-high boots. She appeared on television, often skimpily dressed, in skits for Monty Python *or* Benny Hill, *and was one of the pioneer Page Three girls.*

Flanagan first met the Krays after striking up an unlikely friendship with their beloved mother Violet in a hairdresser's. She would remain firm friends with them until they died, but it was Reggie to whom she was closest. Violet Kray apparently harboured a secret wish to see the two of them married, but though Reggie proposed to her three times and she was sometimes described as his fiancée, Flanagan never officially accepted him, and he went on to marry someone else. The Kray twins were arrested in 1968 and later imprisoned for life for two murders – George Cornell who was shot dead by Ronnie in the Blind Beggar pub in 1966, and Jack 'the Hat' McVitie, who was murdered by Reggie at a party in Hackney in 1967. Ronnie, who was a paranoid schizophrenic, died in Broadmoor, the infamous hospital for the criminally insane, in 1995. Reggie would serve over three decades before being released on compassionate grounds just before he died in 2000. Flanagan now lives in a flat in Hackney, not far from the Krays' old stomping ground. Her walls are crammed with photographs from her modelling days, and pictures of celebrities she has known, including, of course, Ronnie and Reggie. Though fresh from her job working in a local charity shop, on the day we meet she is immaculately dressed, and hardly seems to draw breath for hours on end as she charts her relationship with the most feared men in Britain.

It always amazes me that young kids, who weren't alive when Ronnie and Reggie Kray were sent to prison for life, are still so fascinated by the myth, still buying the T-shirts, still reading the books.

Reggie Kray proposed to me three times. It was in all the newspapers that we were going to be married. I knew him for years before he was arrested and I visited him and Ronnie all through the three decades they were in prison. I was part of that myth. And yet to me it was my reality, it was my life.

I do think I've led a very eventful life and a very fated life. I never regret not marrying Reggie Kray because I wasn't in love with him. But I was always proud I helped them in any way I could because I promised their mother I would. I was sitting on Mrs Kray's bed in the London hospital before she died. She held my hand in front of Charlie Kray and she said, 'Flanagan, promise me you'll carry on visiting the twins when I'm gone.' She died twenty-four hours later. I made that promise and I always honoured that promise.

I don't regret all those years of visiting, but I certainly don't condone what they did. I've never condoned their crimes. I know they were terrifying people, the two of them, very violent. But when it comes to the Krays, I can only speak of how I was treated. I've met a lot of people in my life, but I've never been treated the way Ronnie and Reggie treated me. They treated me like a princess.

I'm not from the East End originally. I'm from Islington, although I was actually born in Hemel Hempstead because I was a war baby. In those days mums-to-be had to be evacuated to give birth. I was born in 1941 while Hitler was bombing London. My mum and I were only in Hemel Hempstead a week, then we came back to Islington to be with my father. My sister and brother came along a few years later.

I had a very good upbringing. We weren't spoiled but we had everything we wanted. We were poor but I can never ever remember being hungry. Meals were at the table all together whether it was a cheap stew or bread and jam and Swiss roll and custard.

My dad was the most handsome man you've ever seen in your life. He was a stonemason from Ireland. He came over here to watch a football match and only intended to stay for a week. But he went to a party, met my mum, who was a little petite cockney from King's Cross, and never went back. He did jobs like labouring, then he went on the railway as a porter and stayed working there until he died. He looked like a film star, did my dad. He used to walk around and tip his hat to the women and they all used to say to my mum: 'How on earth did you get him?'

Believe it or not, I went to a convent school – Our Lady of Sion on the Holloway Road. I had a very authoritarian education and my father was very strict. By four and a half I was able to read and tell the time because my father had sat down and taught me. He had very strong ideas of right and wrong.

My dad died on my fifteenth birthday. He'd been in hospital suffering from heart trouble. I had a few friends over and my mum went up there after we'd all gone to bed, and he died. He was only forty-nine. After he died, I left school immediately to be a hairdresser at the place I'd been working on Saturdays. Again, it was in the Holloway Road. I did a three-year apprenticeship there until I was eighteen. I didn't really have any further ambitions. Then I went to a hair exhibition where there was a photographer taking pictures of all the styles. I had this long blonde hair and he decided to take pictures of me as well as the hair models. After he'd developed them, he rang my mum and said, 'She's very photogenic. She should be a model.'

I was nineteen. I went to this agency who took me on immediately and almost overnight I left the hairdresser's and became a fashion model – walking up and down catwalks, doing shows. It was an amazing experience. I went to New York with Mary Quant. I modelled in Amsterdam and Germany. Hot pants, boots, swimsuits . . . I modelled everything. At twenty, I got married to the local boyfriend I'd been with since I was eighteen. His name was Patrick Flanagan, and after that I became known universally as 'Flanagan' or, more often, 'Flan'.

A year later, I was in a hairdresser's having my hair done when I got chatting to an older lady who turned out to be Violet Kray. I noticed how she was besieged with people asking her to pass on messages to her sons. They were telling her about old people having nasty things put through their letter boxes, or someone's cat being hurt – loads of stuff. The poor woman told me she couldn't go anywhere without being harassed like that, and it had got to the point where she dreaded going out to have her hair done. Well, I didn't know who she was or who her sons were – I assumed they were local businessmen who happened to be really involved with their community – but I felt sorry for her. She was just lovely, a lovely woman.

I said, 'Well, I'm trained as a hairdresser. I could come round to your house to cut your hair.' And she was thrilled. She said, 'You could meet my sons.'

She gave me the address: 178 Vallance Road, Bethnal Green. I didn't even know where the East End was. I'd never been to the East End in my life. I had to have instructions to find Bethnal Green and I'd certainly never heard of the Krays.

I had a little white Mini then (all in all I had twelve different Minis over thirty years). Round I went to Vallance Road. The lovely little old lady I'd met at the hairdresser answered the door and sat me down and gave me tea. Then ten minutes later I was washing her hair and putting her rollers in when then the door opened and this gorgeously handsome, 6 ft 1 blond guy came in. She said, 'This is my son, Charlie.' He was gorgeous, so handsome, was Charlie Kray. I thought: Wow, he's lovely. And he was charming and polite.

I didn't meet Ronnie and Reggie that day. I met them when I went back again a week later. She'd obviously told them to be there. Well, I just couldn't believe it. They were just so identical. You couldn't turn from left to right and tell them apart. Which is why, later on, they'd been able to swap places when Ronnie was in a secure hospital in the late 1950s. Reggie went to visit and just sat down in Ronnie's seat, and then Ronnie got up and left at the end of visiting time. You couldn't tell them apart.

The twins were asking me all these questions about what I did. I told them I used to be a hairdresser but was now modelling. They said, 'Well, if we can help you in any way . . .' I thought: How on earth could these two local businessmen help *me*? Anyway, I didn't need help, I'd conquered the modelling world. I got every job you could imagine. Wherever I went for an audition, if I didn't get the job I was shocked.

It was only when I went home and was talking to my husband's friends one night that I found out who these two polite sons of the sweet old lady really were. 'You've met the Krays!' they all said, completely awestruck. 'You do know who they are, don't you? They rule the East End, they're extremely violent. Ronnie Kray has been considered insane for years.'

I couldn't believe it. I thought they were joking. After

that I used to hear the most dreadful stories of violence and then I'd remember those polite men I always met and think: This can't be the same house I go to, they can't be the same men.

These were two beautifully dressed men who were polite to their mother and came home to change their shirts at six o'clock every day. Do you know, that woman used to do four shirts a day? Two for the morning and two at six o'clock. Imagine that, seven times a week. That's twenty-eight shirts a week she had to wash and iron. I said, 'Violet, you're mad.' She said, 'Oh no, they're very particular about their shirts.' But of course she wanted to do it because she idolised them, especially Ronnie who was her favourite.

All through the 1960s, up until they were arrested in 1968, I spent a lot of time with the Krays. I went to parties with them, they invited me round to the Grave Maurice – a pub in Whitechapel Road – and the Carpenters Arms. They'd take their mother too.

Even though I was married all through my twenties I always thought Reggie liked me. Charlie used to say I was the sister he never had. But Reggie, I always thought, liked me in a different way. But then he was married too, to his first wife, Frances. I went to the wedding. She was a lovely, pretty little thing, but very vulnerable, very fragile.

She didn't know how to handle him and wasn't able to stand any violence or talk of violence. He was very possessive of her. He wouldn't let her go out. She could only go down the road shopping with Mrs Kray. The hairdresser used to come to the house, her clothes were delivered. In the end, she couldn't stand it. She was on medication and she obviously overdosed on it in a very depressed state. It was very sad. He was terribly upset.

After Frances died, Mrs Kray was always trying to set me up with Reggie. That's why she used to take me out with her. I'd say, 'I can't come round on Saturday' and she'd say, 'Well, make it Friday then. Do my hair and then we'll go round and see the boys for an hour.'

I always had a lot of affection for Reggie Kray. I always had this feeling that in a different time and a different place, things could have been different. He was a very attractive man, slightly less bad-tempered than Ronnie, although I wouldn't say he took his orders from Ronnie. He knew exactly what he was doing. But I think if he hadn't been Ronnie's brother, he'd have been a professional boxer. He had that killer instinct in the ring. The other one was just like a slugger, coming in to bash everybody up. Reggie was a very good boxer, he was a good businessman.

As time went on I became more aware of the differences between the twins. If I walked into the pub with Mrs Kray and Reggie was there, she'd smile and he'd wave and come over and buy her a drink. It was all friendly and normal. But the minute the other one walked in the pub, the atmosphere completely changed.

It was like a hush. People who were laughing, stopped laughing, because he used to get into these black moods and think you were laughing at him. He was very volatile, very violent. He had these unbelievable, mesmerising eyes that struck fear into everyone. I never heard Ronnie Kray raise his voice. I've never heard that he raised his voice. He spoke in quite a soft way, almost a twang, that a lot of people thought afterwards was quite effeminate. Of course no one would ever say it in his presence. He would usually bring a young boy with him. The mother, Mrs Kray, never asked any questions, she never mentioned it.

As soon as he'd walk in she'd sigh with contentment and say, 'Oh, Ronnie's here', and I used to think: Why are you happy when he looks as though he could murder someone? He'd come over and nod to his mum and nod to me. If people were crowding around the table, he'd flick his fingers at one of the gang and say, 'Get rid of them, I don't want them round my mother, I don't want them round this table. She's enjoying a night out.'

The old man, Old Charlie, was hardly ever around. He was out on the knocker, going door to door collecting gold, silver, watches to sell. He'd go all over the country. The boys didn't get on with him very well as they got older. I think they sensed a little bit of violence had gone on between the old man and his wife, but of course after the twins were fifteen, the old man had no chance to touch her or even raise his voice. Because one look from Ronnie, even at fifteen or sixteen, would silence him. It would silence anyone.

You know what though? I was never scared of Ronnie. Never. I've met people in my life after that that I'd be wary of, but I was never wary of him. He was always polite and lovely to women. I never heard him swear. No swearing. He couldn't have sworn in front of his mother.

Mrs Kray always referred to Ronnie as a businessman. 'Ronnie's going to open another club,' she'd say. He had the Double R, and Esmeralda's Barn in the West End. That's how they met Lord Boothby, the Conservative MP. He was a West End connection. Boothby sued the *Sunday Mirror* for implying there was a homosexual connection between himself and Ronnie Kray. What rubbish! Ronnie Kray went to Boothby's flat to procure him boys, that's all.

Ronnie was outraged by that rumour. He said, 'He's fat and he's old.' Boothby used to dress in these horrible clothes while Ronnie was all in Italian silk. Ronnie was very particular about how people looked – he'd never have looked at Boothby.

There was one particular young boy who was with Ronnie a lot. I remember seeing him in the Blind Beggar with a Rolex on his wrist. I said to Charlie, 'That's a Rolex.' He said, 'Yeah, it cost a fortune.' But Ronnie was never effeminate or camp. He would never touch the boy. The boy would have to sit there on his chair in the Esmeralda or the Double R. He would drink his drink and stay put. He'd be in a beautiful suit, beautiful shirt. Ronnie would buy him anything. In Broadmoor the boy was the murderer Charlie Smith.

I think Ronnie got his temper and violence from one of his mum's sisters, Auntie Rose, because that temper certainly didn't come from his mother or his father. As far as I know, Auntie Rose encouraged a lot of the thumbing their nose at the law. When the twins were conscripted into the army for two years, some people said it might get rid of their bad tempers, but she knew they'd be back soon enough. And they were. They had a fight with two officers and ran away. They got dishonourably discharged and Auntie Rose was happy. She used to have terrible fights in the streets with women and with men.

I think most of the legend that grew up around the twins at that time stemmed from them being twins. They were split in two, right down the middle. I've sat in Mrs Kray's kitchen with Reggie, and he's said: 'Oh, I've got a terrible headache.' Then a few minutes later, the door would open and Ronnie would walk through the door and say, 'Mum, I've got a terrible headache.' Later I'd visit one of them in prison and he'd say something and the next morning a letter would come from the other saying exactly the same thing. They were absolutely identical until Ronnie was ill and diagnosed with schizophrenia and put on the tablets and he blew up a bit. That's why Georgie Cornell was killed, for calling him a 'fat poof'. If he'd just called him a 'poof' I think that would have been all right.

In their prime they were absolutely identical and they both had terrifying tempers. Instead of fighting one man, you were fighting two. You've had a row with Reggie and all of a sudden Ronnie's appeared and he wants to break your jaw. You had a row with Ronnie and Reggie's appeared. They each had a violent temper, combined with a force of two, with each of them thinking like the other.

I wasn't surprised when I heard about the first murder, George Cornell, who was left dead on the floor of the Blind Beggar pub. To me, Ronnie Kray could have murdered anyone in the state he was in. He was a time bomb waiting to go off. He was on these terrible tablets, he was in a depressive state. He thought nobody could touch him. He thought the police couldn't touch him.

He was obsessed with guns from a young age – Mrs Kray told me that. That's why the twins left home and got a flat nearby because she wouldn't have weapons in the house. Everyone always behaved like gentlemen in Violet's house.

They used to hold meetings upstairs in the house at Vallance Road. Violet would take a tray up with tea and biscuits. Then if we were sat downstairs having cake, Reg would come down and joke, 'Oh I see, you send us up biscuits and keep the cake for yourselves. Where's our cake then?' Later, they'd all come down the stairs one by one and call, 'Bye bye, Mrs Kray.' The last one down would bring back the tray and say, 'Thank you, Mrs Kray.' They all loved her. But while she didn't mind the meetings – 'They're all business-men,' she used to say – she wouldn't allow the weapons in the house, so Ronnie had to have somewhere else to keep them.

What I *was* surprised about was the murder Reggie did. That wasn't supposed to be. Jack McVitie was a nuisance and a scallywag. He used to hit women. He was on pills. He was only taken to that party, I believe, to get a good hiding from Reggie. Reggie pulled out the gun and fired. But the gun didn't go off, therefore Ronnie handed Reggie a knife and the man got stabbed to death trying to run out of the door. No body has ever been found. The Lambrianou brothers who were part of the Firm, were told by Ronnie to 'clear that up'. Charlie Kray, who was in bed fast asleep with his wife at the time, got ten years for it. He wasn't even told about the murder until the next morning.

There were all sorts of myths about where the body ended up. He was fed to the pigs, was one of them. Tony Lambrianou has always admitted the body was rolled up in a quilt and put in the car. He drove to south London and then Freddie Foreman, a former member of the Firm, took over and the body was transferred. The McVitie family has always wanted to know where it was. He did have a wife and he did have kids and sisters and brothers, after all.

It was a volatile time. I noticed Mrs Kray was more tense than usual in the weeks before the twins were arrested in May 1968. I asked her what the matter was and she said: 'I hear people whispering things and there's a terrible atmosphere over the East End that something's going to happen.' Well, happen it did.

At six o'clock one morning, the day after one of my visits to Vallance Road, the twins were arrested in their flat. Reggie was with a girlfriend and Ronnie was with a boy. That police inspector, Nipper Read, had arranged it so that they swooped and arrested a whole load of them all at the same time, all over London, including Charlie Kray.

The trial, at the beginning of 1969, lasted several weeks. I went to the Old Bailey about a dozen times with Mrs Kray. I remember one time I was there the judge, Melford Stevenson, mentioned Frances, Reggie's dead wife, and Reggie started screaming across the court.

I was there in court for the sentence, but Mrs Kray wouldn't go. Couldn't face it. Don't forget Charlie was there in the dock too – all three of her boys facing long prison sentences. Neither of the twins had a wife at the time, so I went.

We knew the sentence was about to be pronounced

because the judge said the day before: 'I've heard everything. I don't want to hear any more.'

In today's world, they'd have got seven years each. In fact, Ronnie would have been sent away for psychiatric assessment, but Reggie would have got seven years.

At the time, we all thought they'd get twenty years, although when I said that to Mrs Kray, she was upset and said, 'Please don't say that.'

I knew by the way Melford Stevenson came out and said, 'In my view society has earned a long rest from your activities,' that it was going to be a political sentence. But I wasn't prepared for how long it was.

They were sentenced to life. The judge said, 'I sentence you to life, and you'll serve a minimum of thirty years.' To say that thing about thirty years, that was political. They wanted to get them off the streets. They wanted to stop organised crime spreading into the West End.

Tony Lambrianou – one of my best friends, who I'd known since I was a teenager – was waiting downstairs at the courthouse while Ronnie and Reggie were being sentenced. Ronnie and Reggie came down the stairs just as the others were getting ready to go up to get their own sentences.

Tony said Ronnie walked down, took a cigarette, lit it – don't forget he'd just got told he was going to spend thirty years in prison, no less – and he looked out of the window and said: 'All right, Tony, you're up next.

Ain't it a lovely day?' It *was* a beautiful sunny day, but he had to be mad, didn't he? To say that after hearing he'd spend the next thirty years in prison?

Tony couldn't believe it. He said, 'I turned to Reggie and said "what did you get?" thinking it must have been a light sentence. Reggie said, "We have to serve thirty years minimum".'

As everyone else came up, I sat there in court and watched them all being sentenced. They were all standing there, the Lambrianous, Freddie Foreman. Freddie got ten years; the Lambrianous got fifteen.

They couldn't give Charlie Kray the same sentence as his brothers, so they sentenced him for disposing of a body, even though he'd been in bed at the time of the murder and they'd never found a body. He got ten years and he served seven. When Charlie was sentenced I felt more sorry for him than anyone else because he hadn't done anything wrong. He wasn't there at either one of the killings. He wasn't a villain. We used to call him Champagne Charlie. He liked the women – and the women certainly liked him. Including Miss Barbara Windsor. He had an affair with her. He really liked her.

After starting off being imprisoned separately, the twins were eventually brought together again at Parkhurst. Mrs Kray was their first visitor. Don't forget she had to visit three sons in prison. She was always taking gifts to the wardens. She used to take her home-made apple pie all the way to Parkhurst, which is on the Isle of Wight – a train and a ferry, and then all the way back.

She always said to me: 'If ever I can't go to see the boys, promise me you'll go to see them.' I said, 'I'll go anyway, just as soon as I'm passed by the Home Office.' She said, 'You will get passed because I've put in a request and so have the boys.'

In the meantime, my career was flourishing. I was doing more and more television. I'd started to do *Monty Python*, *The Two Ronnies*, *Dave Allen*, *The Likely Lads*; I'd been a *Benny Hill* girl three times. I got on very well with Benny Hill. We used to go up to his house in Kensington, about every third Friday I'd take three or four girls with me – models, beautiful girls. He'd say, 'She's nice, Flan, she's chatty.' He liked women with a bit of animation. Don't forget, at five o'clock in the morning you were expected to be running around trees in Acton Park wearing a bikini and boots. You had to have some character to do that.

We'd do it because we wanted to be seen on television. But my first husband didn't like it. He didn't like me doing anything risqué. In the ten years I was with him, I did television and films and swimsuits and leg-work but nothing topless. He would never have stood for that. But when we split up in 1970 I started doing other types of work.

I became a Page Three after being on *Benny Hill*. It was a brand new thing then. They picked two girls to have their pictures taken on the same day – a blonde (me) and a brunette. We each got £12.50. That's all you got in those days. It's funny, I knew Sam Fox since she was a child when her parents occasionally brought her into my husband's pub in Stoke Newington. After she got famous, I asked her how much she got for doing Page Three on her sixteenth birthday. She said, '£250 for the hour. And I always think of you, Flan, with your £12.50.'

At the end of the day Larry Lamb, who was the editor of the *Sun* spread out the pictures in front of him and tried to pick one. Apparently, he said: 'Do you know what? This is going to appear tomorrow morning in the newspaper. The kids are sitting there eating their breakfast before they go to school. We'll go for the angelic-looking one.' That was me. That was how Page Three was conceived at that time. There was nothing dirty about it.

I never forgot my promise to Violet Kray and used to visit Reggie and Ronnie when I could, sometimes with Mrs Kray, sometimes not. She used to say Reggie loved me. She'd say, 'My Reggie has a soft spot for you.' I'd say, 'Oh, Violet, you're just saying that.' She'd say, 'He's always talking about you.' But then men are men. They'll talk about you if you're looking nice or they fancy you; it doesn't mean they love you.

The truth is I loved Reggie Kray, but not in the way I loved my second husband, Terry Cox. He was the love of my life. Terry knew the Krays before they went into prison so they accepted him no problem. It didn't make a difference to them whether I was married or not because they were inside. They were just glad I married someone they knew. I was married to Terry for seven years from 1976 to 1983, but left when he got into cocaine. He'd got in with the wrong crowd, and I had the feeling he was starting to get into drugs. That is so against everything I believe in. I've campaigned against drugs all my life. I've buried two Page Three girls because of drugs, so I certainly wasn't going to be married to someone who was using them. We lived in a beautiful house in Chigwell, but I left with my little boy who was only seven. After we left, my husband had heart problems, probably exacerbated by his cocaine use. He had a heart transplant while still in his early forties and lasted another twenty-two months, but he was still taking cocaine and he eventually died from a fatal heart attack. What a waste. Ron and Reggie sent flowers to the funeral.

But at least I had my son out of that marriage. Everyone calls him JJ. I named him James Jeremy and the nurses couldn't fit it on the little band, so they put JJ and it stuck. Everyone knows JJ. I used to take him everywhere. I took him on jobs, took him to prisons, even took him to Stringfellows and hid him in the toilet so that he could meet Tony Adams, the Arsenal player who I knew was going to be there. I sneaked him in and hid him in the ladies. Sneaked him out when Peter Stringfellow wasn't looking so he could get his autograph. Over the years, JJ came to know all the Page Three girls – Linda Lusardi, Sam Fox, Suzi Mizzi . . .

All the time this was going on, I never stopped visiting the Krays. After seven years, when Charlie came out of prison, we'd sometimes go together. I was visiting Reggie for years. He always wanted me to look lovely. I could never go with trousers. I'd have my hair done and wear lovely, beautiful tailored suits I got from work with stockings and always high heels. He loved it of course – if you've got a roomful of men sitting there with their women and their women don't look anything like the one who's visiting you . . . well, he was really proud. He always said I looked lovely and asked me where I got my clothes. He was quite controlling, mind. He'd say, 'I love your hair – but wear it down next week.'

Whenever I got home I'd get a call from Reggie to make sure I'd got back all right. Don't forget I had to take a ferry and a train back from the prison. Parkhurst was a freezing cold horrible prison. Nice wardens though, but a dreadful place to get to. I used to hate that ferry journey. I don't like water. I can't swim. I'm frightened of water. There used to be a lot of trouble on the ferry sometimes. Later on, I'd sometimes travel there with Sonia Sutcliffe, wife of the Yorkshire Ripper. The things the other wives used to do to her! They'd throw drinks on her, spit on her. They all thought she knew, you see, what her husband was doing (even though she didn't). Their husbands might be in for robbery and violence, but not against women or children.

Even so, I never forgot my promise to Mrs Kray and so I'd go every month to see Reggie and every six weeks to Broadmoor to see Ronnie – he'd been moved there when he got more unstable. Broadmoor is completely different to Parkhurst or the other prisons. Anyone can visit Broadmoor, you just have to sign the book and say what relation you are to the prisoner.

I think that's why Mrs Kray was always so adamant that I should specially visit Reggie. It surprised me at the time because Ronnie was always her favourite. I couldn't understand it, but of course in the end I realised Ronnie Kray was in Broadmoor with a beautiful cell and could order what he wanted to eat, and have any visitor he liked any day, twice a day. He could wear all his own clothes and could take presents and money from people – which he did all the time.

Ronnie had a thing about watches. He had some lovely watches. He was always taking them off people. I'd always say to people, 'Wear a £10 watch when you go to visit Ron. Don't wear anything valuable.' One time, Ronnie asked me to bring Tony Lambrianou to visit, after he'd been released. As we went in I said, 'Tony, what watch are you wearing?' He said, 'The one my parents gave me when I was in prison.' I said, 'Take it off, quick. He'll ask for it.' I put it in my handbag. I took lots of people to visit Ronnie. I took the Kemp brothers. I said, 'Don't wear an expensive watch. He'll ask you for a present.'

I suppose Mrs Kray felt sorry for Reggie, who was in prison uniform and could accept no money or presents, only postal orders for his canteen money. Ronnie Kray had a pork pie in a tin delivered from Harrods every Saturday. In his cell he used to have two other friends. Every Saturday night he'd cut up this pork pie and have lovely cheese and wine. Reggie would have nothing.

When I used to go visiting with Charlie, Charlie would be all lovely – beautiful suit, beautiful tie – but whatever Charlie was wearing, Ronnie would be dressed better. He'd come out and he'd have gold cufflinks with R & R engraved on them. He'd be wearing beautiful rings people had given him, lovely suits and always an expensive watch. He used to have a tailor going in every Christmas to measure him up in case he'd put on an ounce or two, then he'd take delivery of a new suit in January. Beautiful ties, silk shirts. Whatever Charlie wore, he couldn't compete with Ronnie. You'd think Ronnie was the psychiatrist in there.

He'd have these beautiful horn-rimmed glasses. I'd buy them for him and bump into someone who knew him and they'd say: 'How much were those, then?' I'd say, '£25', or whatever. And they'd say, 'I'll pay for them. Just tell him Sam said hello', or Joe or whoever.

Then he'd send me down Mile End Road to the tie shop. Ronnie would say, 'I want six silk ties.' 'What do you want them for?' I'd ask. 'I'm giving them to the wardens as presents.' He was very generous, was Ronnie Kray – much more so than his brothers – but then he never knew the value of money. He was like a little child. Everything he earned in Broadmoor he gave away. He had no concept of how much things were worth. I remember telling him a loaf of bread was fifty pence. He said, 'What is fifty pence?' He never got past crowns and shillings.

I had to go to Denmark Street once to buy him an electric guitar. I'd made the mistake one day of telling him that Denmark Street was the place where Eric Clapton and Bill Wyman and Pete Townshend bought their guitars. Next thing I knew Ronnie said, 'Go to that shop.' The money was left in an envelope for me at Broadmoor's signing-out office. I said, 'I don't know anything about electric guitars.' He said, 'Just ask the man for the sort of guitar he would sell to Eric Clapton.'

I said, 'But who's it for?' I thought he'd taken up the electric guitar. But of course it was for the boy, Charlie Smith. Beautiful, he was. Blond hair. Looked like James Dean but with long hair. In there for murder.

I went to the guitar shop with Charlie Kray and I

said to the man behind the counter: 'You do deliver, don't you?' He said, 'Yes, madam.' I said, 'Well, I may as well tell you, it's to go to Broadmoor.' He looked a little surprised but he brought a guitar for me to look at. 'And whom do we address it to, madam?' he asked. I said, 'Mr Ronnie Kray.' Then the man looked at Charlie and said, 'You're the older brother aren't you?' Well, from that point on they couldn't do enough for us. They were scurrying around, getting a lovely box. I said, 'Well, how much is this guitar?' The man said, '£350, madam'. I said, 'I've only got £300.' He said, 'Done.' I said, 'It has to be delivered two days before Christmas.' 'No problem, madam, and we'll waive our delivery charge.' That's the kind of reaction you'd get.

I used to go to this shirt shop in Jermyn Street. I'd go in there and the assistant would say: 'Hello, dear. Ronnie, sixteen and a half neck, isn't it?' I'd say, 'But how . . .' and she'd say: 'Oh, we've had a telephone call. He wants one blue, one white, and he said the lady would come in to pick them up and bring them to him next visit.' They were lovely shirts too. Irish linen. He organised everything from his cell. You'd see the other inmates in Broadmoor with coffee stains and bits of food all over them. Ronnie was something else. When you went to visit, he'd always come out ten minutes late, so that everyone would be seated and looking at him. And he was always so beautifully dressed. You could put your make-up on in the shine of his shoes.

Poor Reggie, he could wear jeans or trackbottoms and that blue and white shirt. They used to have to wear shoes but in the end they changed it so they could wear trainers. Reggie didn't know a decent pair of trainers was £70. I'd go into the pub and talk to different people and say, 'I've got to get Reggie a pair of trainers to take in next week' and they'd say, 'Here's £20', or 'Here's £10' and I'd get enough to pay for them. So you have to believe that in their early life the twins did a lot of good, because people wouldn't have continued supporting them for thirty years otherwise.

In the early 1980s, two things happened to change how things were with me and Reggie. Firstly I left my husband because of the drugs. Also Mrs Kray died. That had a huge effect on Reggie.

The first marriage proposal was almost jokey. When I used to go to visit Reg, there was one guard who would always arrive with loads of paperwork under his arm. I had to apply for parole for Reggie every year – write letters – and of course you always got refused, but it didn't matter, you still did it, so he'd bring it all with him. This warden was very nice – Mrs Kray used to make apple pies for him. He used to come in and put his tea and coffee down and say, 'Oh, I see you've got your lovely lady visiting you again, Reg?' And Reggie would go: 'Yes, isn't she lovely? Don't you like how she's done her hair?' Silly things. He would see other prisoners looking at me, and they'd have wives and girlfriends kissing them, mums kissing him – and Reggie didn't have his mum to visit after Mrs Kray died. The guard would say: 'When are you two getting married? You should get married, Reg. That'd give you something to look forward to in here.' I used to look across to him and laugh and say: 'You won't be getting married any more, will you, Reg?' But I think he used to go back to his cell and think about it.

Then I'd go to Broadmoor and Ronnie would say, 'You know, you should marry my Reggie. You'd be very good for him. You'd get him parole.' I used to reply, 'Well, I apply every year to the Home Office for parole for the two of you as it is.'

Ronnie would say: 'Don't bother applying for parole for me any more. I'm never coming out.' He knew he was never coming home. He said: 'Forget about me. Apply for Reggie.'

So I started applying for parole for Reggie and saying I was the fiancée, Reggie's fiancée. Ronnie Kray wanted me to marry Reggie. He used to write to him: 'Marry Flanagan. Why don't you propose to Flanagan?'

The second time Reggie asked me to marry him, there'd been a joke going round right before I visited. All the other prisoners had been asking, 'Why don't you propose to her today, Reg?' And when I walked in, one looked to the other – a big visiting hall with about twenty tables – and then they all started humming 'Here comes the bride'. I thought: What are they doing that for? Then Reggie came in and they all called out, 'Here's the bridegroom.'

I had a friend from the East End with me that day, and my son JJ. Reg said: 'They've all been singing, putting notes through my door, and warning me they're going to start singing that and saying, "You should marry her. She'd be good for you."' Then he looked at my son and said: 'How do you fancy me as a stepdad?' The thing was, he didn't even look at me, it was straight to my son. My little boy was used to visiting both the Krays. JJ said, 'Yeah, that'll be all right, Reggie,' Reggie went on: 'You be a good boy. Are you in a youth club? You continue with your boxing', and all this. Then finally, he looked at me and said: 'Well, what about it, shall we get married?'

I was really taken aback. I said, 'You can't marry someone you don't love.' And he said, 'Who said I don't love you? I've always loved you. My mum loved you and my brothers love you.' I said: 'I'm not marrying them, what about you?' He said, 'I've always loved you.'

I just laughed and changed the subject. Then six months later I walked in and they all started singing again. The guard was laughing, saying: 'You've got a surprise today.' When I sat down, Reggie said, 'Right, no more beating about the bush now. I'm going to get married.' I said, 'Well, who are you getting married to?' I thought he had another woman, because he had lots of visitors. He said, 'What are you talking about? I'm going to marry you. My two brothers are driving me mad. Everyone in here is driving me mad. They all say I should marry you.' I made a joke when the guard came. I said, 'He's proposed, but where is my ring?' He started laughing then and again I changed the subject because I didn't really know what to say.

At eight thirty the next morning, there was a knock on the door of the house I was living in in Victoria Park, and there was Charlie Kray with a caravan made of matchsticks, the kind they make in prison. He said, 'I've been told I have to be here at half eight to give you this present from Reggie.' I said, 'Is that instead of a ring? I want a diamond ring, I don't want a caravan made of matchsticks.' He said, 'He's sat down for a month to make that.' I said, 'Yeah, but I still want a ring.'

So Charlie said, 'He knows that you're going to court on Friday for your divorce and he's sending half of Fleet Street there so that they can meet his fiancée. I said, 'He's in prison. How can he do that?' But of course, he could do anything from his cell. He'd rung all the papers – the *Sun*, *Mirror*, *Mail*, *Standard*, *Star*. He'd said: 'I'm getting engaged. She'll be at the divorce court in the Strand, Friday morning to divorce her husband, and then I'm going to marry her.'

I didn't really believe it and forgot all about it. So on the Friday I went to the divorce court with my two girlfriends. As we came out to go for a nice lunch to celebrate, there were all these photographers there. I couldn't understand it, I thought someone famous must be getting divorced – a film star like Elizabeth Taylor. They all started shouting out, 'Flan! Flan!' They all knew me from the modelling, see. They were all shouting, 'We hear you're going to marry Reggie.'

I said: 'Who said that? I didn't say yes. I just asked for a ring.'

The guy from the *Sun* said, 'If you marry him, Flan, you know you'll have to marry him in handcuffs in prison.' He wouldn't be allowed out for the wedding as he still had fifteen more years to serve.

I replied: 'Oh well, at least I'll know where he is at night.' That was the headline in all the papers. It was in seven newspapers, even *The Times*. 'Model to marry Kray Twin. She says: "At least I'll know where he is at night."'

We eventually got away, after they got me to say that I'd wait until the following week's visit to see if he came up with an engagement ring. The next week I went to see Reggie and he asked: 'What do you want an engagement ring for? You've got a beautiful ring on your finger from your second husband.' I said: 'I want another one.' He said, 'But you haven't said "yes" yet.'

The truth is I was thinking of all the running around Mrs Kray had done over the years, which killed her. It definitely killed her. And all the running around I'd done myself with the twins. I thought: Do I really want my name to be Kray? My son would always be called Cox, but he'd have Reggie Kray as a stepfather and you never know what that might do to a little boy, how it might affect him at school. I talked to my sister and brother and was thinking: Do I really want this for another fifteen years? I'd be toing and froing. I wouldn't even be young any more by the time he got out.

I didn't mind doing the parole letters and putting on the functions they asked me to do to raise money, but it was all the other stuff I was worried about. When Ronnie was married to Kate Kray, she used to get calls all the time. You'd never know if he was going to overdose or anything so she couldn't turn her phone off.

But I didn't want all that. I'd been visiting prisons every month for fifteen years and it was enough for me. The next time I went to visit, Reggie didn't mention the marriage thing and I knew it was because I kept harping on about the ring, so I thought I just wouldn't bring it up. And it sort of died away after that, even though I carried on visiting just the same as before.

I took JJ to visit both Kray brothers between the ages of seven and twelve. Ronnie would always tell him: 'Don't take drugs, get off the streets, don't join a gang.' He'd say: 'You don't want to end up in here like me, do you?' And always: 'Look after your mother. She's your best friend.' JJ would say, 'No, I'm good, aren't I, Mum?'

Same thing with Reggie: 'You look after your mum,'

he'd tell him. Mum was the fixation of their lives. I think they treated women as well as they did purely because of their mum, because she was a woman. Every woman was potentially someone's mum and every child was somebody's little child.

Women and children in need always affected them. I was forever taking money to the Repton boys' club from Ronnie and Reggie. They did lots of charity work to send dying children to Disneyland. One time Ronnie saw a picture in the paper of an old lady who'd been mugged. He couldn't fathom it at all. He told me to ring up the *Daily Mirror*, get the address and send her £10. She wrote to him at Broadmoor. 'I got your £10. Thank you Ronnie Kray. That's one good deed you've done.'

Hardship stories got to them. I'd say, 'So and so has lost her husband, she's got three kids.' They'd say, 'Send her £20.' So they couldn't have been 100 per cent evil, could they? That's not to say they didn't do evil deeds, mind. I never condoned them killing those men. Those men were somebody's dad, somebody's brother, somebody's son.

After Ronnie died in 1995, we were all frightened to go to see Reggie. Poor Charlie Kray had to go the next morning. He said he was in a terrible, terrible state. But then Reg threw himself into organising the funeral. He started ringing me up saying "right Flan, you've got to be my eyes for this funeral."

I had to organise all the flowers just so. He wanted a boxing ring in flowers on the top of the first car – one glove laying up, one glove laying down, and that was to say 'To Ron from Reg'. Then on the right hand side of the funeral car, in writing, he wanted 'To the other half of me', and another wreath on the horse and carriage saying: 'Colonel'.

I thought 'that's going to be expensive'. I had to go to the prison and get that money and take it to the florist. Then there were Charlie's wreaths, then the cousins' wreaths, then the 26 limos following the horse and carriage, all over Bow Flyover, all through Walthamstow. If you think you saw something when Jade Goody died, you can treble that.

Reggie organised Ronnie's funeral from his cell and he did it unbelievably. People said they'd never seen anything like it since Churchill's funeral. I seated all the people at the church. I had it all on a list from Reggie where he wanted everyone to be seated. He picked the pall bearers, the music, the flowers. Nobody could sit on a seat that wasn't allotted to them. He'd ring people and say: "When you go in, you're to sit where Flanagan puts you. She's got the book of where everyone is to be seated. It's on my orders."

He knew there'd be groupies who wanted to say they'd been to Ronnie Kray's funeral so I had Dave Courtney with 100 security guards to patrol it. There were security guards on the gates, leading up to the door of the Church. And, of course, the whole of Bethnal Green was crawling with police. There was a helicopter following us all the way to Chingford. They were thinking Reggie was going to try to escape. He said "Are they mad?" I was nervous but it was so well organised, I knew no one was going to come in that church who wasn't supposed to because of the guards.

Reggie had to come first. He arrived handcuffed in a van with two police escorts. He had to come in through a side door first and sit in the front row. I filled the church up according to the plan, then as the music played, the coffin came in. Six men from the four corners of London carried the coffin – Freddie Foreman from the South, Charlie Kray from the East End, Alec Stein and Teddy Dennis from the West End, Johnny Nash from North London and their oldest friend Laurie O'Leary.

By this time Reggie had been transferred to Maidstone Prison. On one of my visits there in 1996, I went with a woman called Roberta who'd been writing to Reggie and was going to meet him.

On the way there, we talked and she asked me why I'd said no when Reggie proposed. I told her: 'I really don't want to be a prison wife. I don't mind being a prison visitor, but I don't want to be a prison wife. As a visitor, if I don't want to go one time, I don't go. But a wife has got to go. If she doesn't go one time, the next time there'll be a row.'

After that, Reg told me casually over the phone a couple of times that Roberta had been to visit him by herself on the train. That was all right. Then the next thing I knew, they were engaged.

I started laughing. I rang up Charlie and said: 'What do you think about this Roberta?' He said: 'She's a dark horse, that one.'

I said, 'If he wants to marry her, let him marry her.' And he did. They got married in Maidstone. The best man was an inmate, Bradley Allardyce. Charlie didn't go to the wedding.

But I wasn't jealous. I have no jealousy. I've never known the word. I wasn't jealous when I was working as a model, even when I was surrounded by the most beautiful girls. I've made films with gorgeous women. I did a film with Ursula Andress and I thought she was fabulous. I did a scene with Raquel Welch. We were rowing on a boat topless and she was wearing a brown leather bikini. She was absolutely beautiful – those legs, those boobs, beautiful tawny hair. We were all top models and looking at her thinking how gorgeous she was. It would never have crossed my mind to think: Why aren't I her? I've worked with Charlton Heston, Joan Collins, Tony Curtis, but I've never known jealousy.

Reggie died in 2000 from cancer of the bladder. The last time I saw him was in Wayland Prison in Norwich two months before he died. He looked dreadful and could hardly walk. I knew the application had gone in that day for his compassionate release. I said: 'Reg, they're going to grant it.' He said, 'I don't think so, they'll make me suffer.' I said: 'No. They're going to grant it.'

Of course he should have been released when he'd served thirty years but they still kept him there for another two years. Sent him from Maidstone to Wayland.

That last visit, I cuddled him and gave him a kiss. I knew I wouldn't see him again and it was a really sad occasion. Reggie gave me a letter to an old friend in the East End who he wanted to visit him. He knew he was dying. He knew it was the end. All I took away with me was this letter, sealed, to take to Jack.

When the doctors gave Reggie six weeks to live, he was released, but at first he was released to a hospital. No one was allowed to visit. Then from the hospital he went to the Town House Hotel in Norwich. I've stayed there since. I was talking to the people who owned it. They said if anyone came in to visit while Reggie was there, they had to phone up to Roberta to see if those people were allowed up. Even his old friends who'd been with him for decades, like Freddie Foreman and Mad Frank Faser, had trouble gettingg in to see him.

Reggie died there In that hotel room. I didn't even try to visit. I didn't know If I'd have been allowed through the door. I thought: I've got all my memories. I've had all those years. He knew what I was made of and always treated me with great respect and affection.

It was a very emotional day, Reggie's funeral. We knew it was the last brother as Charlie had died just a few months before. There would never be another funeral like it. I think it was the saddest of the funerals – because it was the last brother and because there was a lot of fuss over the pall bearers.

I know the pall bearers who should have carried that coffin. They were members of the Firm – old, old friends. Roberta wanted Bradley Allardyce from prison and Tony Mortimer who was a member of the pop group East 17 and who'd been visiting Reggie for a few years. All these young people. She didn't want Freddie Foreman and his son Jamie. I asked her why not. She said, 'He broke away from all that stuff two years before he died.' And then she said, 'I don't want any villains. I don't want it to be a Ronnie Kray funeral.' I said: 'No, it's a *Reggie* Kray funeral and he *was* a villain. He murdered someone and he served thirty years for it. But that's not to say that the East End don't want his old friends to carry him. They do.'

As far as I'm concerned, Freddie Foreman and his son Jamie should have carried that coffin. Tony Lambrianou should have carried that coffin. Teddy Dennis should have carried that coffin.

That funeral symbolised the end of an era. The last of the Kray twins to go. There'll never be another pair like them.

FLANAGAN

Of course the myth will go on because the young-sters are still reading the books, watching the films. To me though, they weren't a myth, they were real. They were Ronnie and Reg – Mrs Kray's sons.

ACKNOWLEDGEMENTS

I'd like to thank Stephen Breen of the *Belfast Telegraph* and Else Kvist of the *East London Advertiser* for all their help. Also Bernard O'Mahoney, Jason Marriner, Wensley Clarkson, Barrie Tracey, Charlie Seiga, Graham Johnson and Paul Knight for their generous advice. I'm grateful to Ebury Press and Perseus Books and to Nick Johnston at Quercus. Special thanks to David Griffin and Sarah Tovey on the Costa del Sol.

PICTURE CREDITS